Poppy Cannon's All-Time, No-Time, Any-Time Cookbook

Poppy Cannon's

All-Time,
No-Time,
Any-Time
Cookbook

by Poppy Cannon

THOMAS Y. CROWELL COMPANY
NEW YORK *Established 1834*

Designed by Ingrid Beckman

Manufactured in the United States of America

ISBN 0–690–00263-7

1 2 3 4 5 6 7 8 9 10

Library of Congress Cataloging in Publication Data

Cannon, Poppy.
    Poppy Cannon's all-time, no-time, any-time cookbook.

    1. Cookery. I. Title. II. Title: All-time, no-time, any- time
cookbook.
TX715.C217 1974   641.5   74-12124
ISBN 0-690-00263-7

This book is for my treasured friend, mentor, and good, long-time, well-beloved editor and Boss-Man, Henry Sell, who taught me to know the difference between casual and careless, and made me aware of the elegance of simplicity—on many planes.

New York, April 12, 1974

By Way of Acknowledgments...

Every page and every recipe in this book breathes a thank-you to my family, friends, and neighbors in West Redding, Connecticut, and Manhattan and to the hosts of hosts across the world who have gone a-hunting for me. Literally hundreds have suggested, culled, shared, and served these ideas and discoveries. They have even offered themselves as intrepid testers of my wildest experiments.

I owe a special gratitude to maybe a thousand people in the food and wine world who have supplied me with all kinds of knowledge and information—technical and otherwise.

Always I shall be grateful to the readers who, over the years, have taken the time and trouble to write me, often in great detail, about recipes and their experiences with them. Their letters have brought fresh light to our common problems and led me often in new directions.

Now: a big grateful hug for Elsie Miller, who was a practitioner of our new ways long before we met. She has eagle-eyed and put together skillfully, patiently, the thousands of jigsaw bits and pieces that—Eureka!—make a cookbook come to life.

Contents

Foreword

This book might have been called the timeless cookbook.

Because it is designed especially with time in mind and with the knowledge that time is the most precious commodity in our day and age—perhaps in *any* day and age.

Digging a little deeper, this book of timeless recipes is geared to the proposition that beyond the ever-changing aspect of all worlds—including the culinary—there is a deep, wide ripple of continuity. All the arts, gastronomical and otherwise, are nurtured by tradition. Over the years the best prevails.

A knowledge (as well as a knowledgeable irreverence) of the past might be considered an earmark of any important contribution in a great many fields, epicurean and otherwise.

Much has happened since the first *Can Opener Cookbook* lifted the lid off a whole new world of cooking.

It has been said that there is nothing so vigorous as a sound idea that has found its time. In most instances, that precise time is somewhat *before* the general public is fully aware of it.

Howls of surprise, a good deal of righteous anger and disbelief marked the *Can Opener Cookbook*'s debut. The president of the publishing firm insisted for many months that the book could not come out with "that awful title." "People would be ashamed," he said. "We'd have to sell it in plain brown wrappings."

After firm, energetic persuasion, the sales department was able to convince him.

Never has a cookbook stirred up so much rumpus. Happily, many were impressed—some said "refreshed"—by a new point of view. Others shrieked. The critic at *France-Amérique* wrote acidly that a can opener would not be an open sesame to delight and warned portentously that the *ouvre-boîte* could never be considered a magic wand. According to that commentator, the only miracle worker was, as it always had been, an old wooden spoon.

Nevertheless the book took off, chugging merrily along over the years through three face-lifts and a dozen updatings. From the very beginning, the term *can opener* was—and still is—used generically, almost symbolically, to refer to tools, ingredients, and methods that could be practically guaranteed.

This book, made up of nuggets from the original *Can Opener Cookbook* as well as the *New* and *New/New*; the *Frozen Foods Cookbook*, and the *Electric Epicure*, includes recipes, ideas, suggestions and—what is every bit as important—a philosophy to take into the kitchen.

It concerns itself with the food, the moods, and the moot problems of right here and now. We have tried to bring together in one volume an inspirational trove of information: know-how and know-what about foods in tins and packages, frozen foods in various stages of preparation, and revolutionary techniques. Some recipes make use of newly developed gadgets, appliances and equipment. Others deal with "convenience foods" provided by nature. An egg, for instance, is a prime example; so are a banana, an apple, a piece of cheese.

Through the ages man has developed an incalculable wealth of lore and wisdom concerning delightful ways to deal with natural bounty. Often, the simple ancient knowledge has been supplanted by methods unduly complicated. In this book you will find a number of instances where we have returned to basic simplicity. Take our way with fresh asparagus—laid three layers deep in a shallow pan with a covering of cold water. No lid. You boil ever so briefly and then allow it to stand off-heat so that the process continues to the moment of truth and *holds* perfection. The water itself provides an impeccable thermostat. We thought we had invented this wild-sounding method. Sometimes we were faintly apologetic in the face of unbelieving stares. Then a young student from Burma told us that her family does it the same way. So did her grandmother and her ancestors for a thousand years.

In this case we didn't realize. ... But at other times we were well aware that many of the most surprising ideas, also ideals, of excellence have their roots in many lands and cultures.

Moreover, we have learned in the last decade that older lands have followed us into the realm of processed food. France, England, Germany, Israel, and Egypt, from whom we borrow so much, are vying with us. In some cases they are becoming lands of the mix, the jar, the frozen-food package, and the ubiquitous can opener.

Our Recipe Format

We do not suggest (or expect) that this be your only cookbook, though it might well be your introduction to the art of cooking. So we have made no attempt to cover in our recipes the whole field of cookery. There is, however, a representative collection of recipes in various categories and a sufficient number of each—appetizers, soups, meats, vegetables, salads, desserts, and beverages—to equip you for any occasion. Armed with these recipes and ideas, you should achieve with the least possible expenditure of work and tension not only excellent eating but also considerable acclaim.

Every recipe includes a shortcut—a canned or quick-frozen food, a mix, or a new and simplified way to arrive at a particularly delectable result. In each case we have tried with a few lines of introduction to explain our reasons for including that particular recipe. We have tried also to describe as well as words can the appearance and flavor of the various dishes. Far too many fine recipes are printed to rest unknown, unnoticed, and untasted within the covers of a book simply because modern authors lack the perspicacity of those old-time ladies who more often than not would title their handwritten recipes not merely "Veal Loaf," for instance, but "Aunt Mame's Special Veal Loaf—very light and fluffy." They might add, "Men of this family have always loved a loaf fixed this way with a hard-boiled egg in the center. . . ."

You Will Need:

At least half the social and culinary success of any hurried epicure depends upon a good stock of supplies. The ability to whip up something wonderful with seemingly miraculous speed and ease often depends more on skill in shopping and management than on skill in cooking. In this book we have confined our recipe ingredients to those products that for the most part can be secured in any ordinary grocery store or delicatessen in small as well as big towns and cities.

Among those products called for most frequently in this book and which it would be well to keep on hand—in addition to the ordinary salt, pepper, milk, bread, and butter—are: a collection of canned soups, such as cream of chicken, mushroom, consommé, to be used not only as soups but also in making sauces; canned meats and fish to suit your fancy; canned or quick-frozen chicken, chicken fricassee, and chicken à la king; canned tomatoes, tomato sauce, and tomato paste; your favorite canned or quick-frozen vegetables; oil, vinegar, and prepared salad dressings; cheese, of course; dehydrated vegetable flakes, such as onion flakes, parsley flakes, mixed vegetable flakes; mixes for pastry, rolls, and cookies, as well as cakes, pies, and puddings (vanilla-, chocoate-, and custard-flavored puddings are always good to have on hand); and "storable" milk—evaporated, dehydrated, or condensed.

A Treasury of Seasonings

And then the core of all epicurean effort is a treasury of seasonings. You will want all the usual spices, herbs, and flavorsome seeds such as salt, pepper, cloves, nutmeg, cinnamon, allspice, ginger, curry, sage, marjoram, thyme, basil, tarragon, savory, rosemary, paprika, and monosodium glutamate (generally known under various trade names, such as Accent, Zest, etc.) —and a few of the less usual ones, too, such as cumin, saffron, cardamom, turmeric—condiments, olives, and pickles to be used not only at the table but in preparation of food; extracts over and beyond the usual vanilla. Kitchen Bouquet or some other condiment with a caramelized sugar base adds rich, homemade color to stews and gravies.

Wine Is Fine

Wines also are used frequently—red and white table wines, sherry, port, an occasional dash of champagne, rum, and brandy for that glorious and ever-so-easy and dramatic trick of serving food flambé.(afire).

Although much of your success in contriving the distinguished dish from a ready-to-serve product will depend upon seasoning as well as presentation, it is wise to be light-handed with spices. A good rule is to add at first when seasoning to taste only about half the amount of seasoning you think will be required, and then, tasting as you go, add bit by bit until the result satisfies you.

Wine is most helpful in glamorizing simple dishes and simple meals, but here, too, be cautious as to the amounts used and careful also as to the quality. When improvising your own recipes, add half as much wine as you think you'll need. Taste frequently as you add to be sure the wine will not overpower all other flavors.

Remember that wine is flavoring—that the flavoring is very often one of the least expensive ingredients of the dish as well as the most important. Perhaps it would be best to forget the terms *cooking wine* or *cooking sherry.* The wines you use in cooking need not be expensive but they should be well flavored and well made. The same holds true for other liquors—brandy, rum, liqueurs, and cordials. Cooking with wine need not be expensive when you consider how easy it is to open a bottle beforehand, add wine to the sauce, the soup, the stew, or the fish, and drink the rest with dinner.

Fire and Fame

In a number of instances we have suggested the simple drama of serving ordinary foods flambé. Too many people feel that such theatrics should be confined to the Christmas pudding or an occasional cherries jubilee, but a number of famous restaurateurs have led the procession and now all manner of foods, from appetizers through soups, meats, fish, puddings, and ices, acquire a new attractiveness as well as a definite mellowing and blending of flavors by the addition of some type of spirits, which we suggest should be slightly warmed before being set afire.

At Serving Time

A chef does not serve a dish—he presents it, and his presentation is every bit as important as his preparation. Much of the difference between just cooking and epicurean cooking is the difference in the way the food is served. In our effort to lift quickly prepared food to extraordinary heights of appeal we have in most cases appended a few lines to the recipes titled "At Serving Time," which tell you how to serve, how to garnish attractively and with originality, and in many cases, what to serve with each particular food for an interesting, well-balanced meal. Present-day menus have become so simple. Individual and family likes and dislikes are so varied that we find it much more helpful to have suggestions for "what goes with what" instead of a full-scale formal menu plan.

The Quick Gourmet Meal ... How to Plan It

If methods of cooking have changed in recent years—and they have, enormously—this change is slight compared to the revolution in menus. A family dinner as prescribed in the notable *White House Cookbook* in the early 1900's consisted of approximately a dozen different items, at least four courses, three or four different desserts—not including coffee.

Now even for company three courses are considered lavish. Two-course meals—without an opener—are universally acceptable and in many cases we dine, as well at lunch, on one main dish, nibbling at the fruit centerpiece for dessert or content with "just coffee, please." Planning the meal is no longer a problem of "leading up to and away from" the pièce de résistance, as it used to be, but rather it is a question of combining the right flavors, colors, textures, as well as getting the proper amount of nourishment.

Here, as in planning the most elaborate meals, the same basic rules should be observed. First, there must be contrast—contrast in texture, in color, and in flavor. A smooth and creamy dish must be served along with something crisp; chicken à la king, for example, goes well inside a ring of julienne potato sticks. Crunchy rolls, nuts, carrot sticks, all offer interesting texture contrast to soft foods. You would not follow creamed chicken with a creamy dessert. Contrast in color is equally important— green peas, sliced tomato, golden corn, the rich brown of a grilled lamb chop; a bright green sprinkle of parsley, a cool yellow lemon slice, and chopped egg on black bean soup; the paleness of peas, a scarlet plum, a vivid apricot, a pale and sunny slice of pineapple in a fruit compote. Such things illustrate the possibilities of color contrasts to provide appetite appeal.

Contrast in flavors is even more important. Bland food requires a piquant accompaniment—a pork chop, for example, or other rich meat such as ham or goose is at its best with something cool and fruity, such as applesauce or pickled peaches. Sometimes flavor contrasts—sweet and sour, bland and spicy—are combined in a single dish. More often they accompany or follow each other. A hot curry is ringed with rice and served with a number of sharply contrasted accessories—there's cold beer to sip with curry or chili con carne, followed by fresh fruit.

Drama at the Table

If your food is basically good and if you have contrast in texture, color, and flavor, that's more than half the battle. Add drama and you're sure to make yourself a reputation. All of us in our lifetime have eaten honest, nourishing food that was dull as dishwater.

Drama enters not only in your choice of dishes, silverware, and centerpiece but also in the napkins, the tablecloth or place mats, the color of the candles, the color and shape of the water glasses. All these things can add tremendously to the enjoyment of a meal.

Use your color sense, your creative imagination, when you buy table linens or place mats. Do not be bound by tradition. Dare to dye an old white damask tablecloth a bright shocking pink, a deep leaf green, or a wine red. Have the courage to use a pink plate on that deep green or red cloth. Consider the possibilities of drapery or curtain material as a tablecloth or runner. If you fear the effect of too much washing on the pattern you might try covering the cloth itself with a clear plastic—but not for formal meals!

Be equally imaginative about the centerpiece. No law compels you to use a brace of candles and a low arrangement of florist flowers. A row of potted geraniums might be far more interesting when you serve a great tureen of party soup. And the centerpiece need not always be dead center. Try the effect of a decorative grouping along one side of the table when there are only three to dinner, or place it at the end of a long buffet.

For those times when you particularly want a meal to be "a production," you might plan the menu around some particularly effective dish or accessory in your possession. If you have a huge French casserole make it a point to collect several interesting specialties that can be cooked and served en casserole. Is a beautiful salad bowl a prized possession? Make it a habit to include in your menus a number of main-dish salads. Perfect your skill as a salad impresario and mix the dressing at the table.

Have you a chafing dish? a crêpes suzette pan? a cut-glass punch bowl? Keep them in mind when you begin to think: "What shall we have to eat?" And don't be self-conscious about repeating your specialties or even your menus. Many a fine restaurant and many a clever hostess have built reputations on a few excellent dishes. If you share the almost universal necessity to be host or hostess as well as cook, learn a few tricks of the métier. Always allow yourself at least ten minutes alone in the kitchen before dinner is announced. There are various ways guests can be kept happy during this brief interval—with cocktails and canapés or appetizers, television, or conversation.

Unless you are exceedingly deft and sure of yourself, you may find it wiser to dispense with the first course or to provide one that can properly be set on the table before the guests are called. Make every effort to have by your side either a commodious coffee table or a three-tiered serving table on which extra dishes, accessories, serving spoons, and the like may be set. With a little planning you should be able to arrange matters so that once having sat down to the table, you need disappear only once, just before the dessert.

Whenever you plan a meal, just for your family or for company, don't attempt too much. Keep it simple—confine your efforts to one or two dishes and make them very, very good.

No matter how simple it is, never try out a new dish on a new audience. Even the greatest of chefs has a dress rehearsal before an important dinner.

Serve cold foods cold, chilled foods like salad on plates that have been chilled in the refrigerator, cold drinks preferably in glasses that have previously been filled with ice, frozen desserts on cold plates, too. All this, though it may sound slightly troublesome, is not at all difficult once you become accustomed to the idea. The bowl of salad greens, for example, all washed, dried, and ready for tossing, can go into the refrigerator on top of a pile of salad plates.

Serve hot foods hot. If you have no warming oven (our grandmothers were rather more blessed than we are in this respect, what with the old coal range and the warm oven that hung above it) you can use any oven as a warming oven. Keep the temperature somewhere between 150° and 200° F.—a temperature that should not harm china or silver dishes but will keep plates, serving pieces, coffee and tea cups properly heated. If you are broiling steak or chops and your oven is too hot for the plates, you might use a good-sized top-of-the-stove ovenette such as is sold for baking potatoes, etc. Put an asbestos pad under it and have the heat very low. A steak platter may be warmed on top of the stove on an asbestos pad over a very low flame.

To keep your food at its best for second servings you would be wise to invest in some kind of warming equipment. There are a number of inexpensive and attractive warmers on the market on which ordinary serving pieces and casseroles, of course, may be placed. Most use stubby candles—something like votive candles. Ideal, of course, are thermostatically heated electric warming trays, which come in many sizes.

Openers and Snacks

Showcase—inspiration, source of satisfaction—these opening foods, cocktail accompaniments, and before-dinner appetizers are easy to make, delicious, zestfully flavored, and unusual enough to evoke festive feelings, as well as those admiring *oh*'s and *ah*'s and *m-m-m*'s that break the social ice more effectively than many cocktails.

You will find here only a very few canapés or tidbits that are individually concocted and none that requires finicky decorating. We suggest that your cocktail party guests do most of the work right at the party—and have a fine time in the process!

Any or all of these appetizers may be served before dinner or as party snacks. However, it is a good idea to serve only the simplest appetizers before dinner. More dramatic efforts, such as flaming cabbages, and the hot appetizers, are most appropriate for parties.

READY-MADE PIZZA

Frozen cocktail-size pizzas may be uplifted in the same way.

YOU WILL NEED:

1 quick-frozen pizza	Parmesan cheese
Olive oil	Oregano or basil (optional)

Brush pizza with olive oil. Sprinkle generously with freshly grated Parmesan cheese. If desired, add a bit of oregano or basil. Reheat in the oven.

At Serving Time:

Cut into small pieces as a cocktail, soup, or salad accompaniment, or cut into good-sized wedges like pie and serve as a main dish with red wine, a green salad, and a huge bowl of fruit for dessert.

FROZEN CHEESE ALEXANDRA

Unusual and very, very good is a molded frozen cheese served with hot-out-of-the-oven toast—an unforgettable combination.

YOU WILL NEED:

1/2 pound butter or margarine
1/4 pound Roquefort or blue cheese
2 tablespoons dry sherry or brandy
2 teaspoons minced chives or parsley
Toasted rye bread or whole-wheat
  Melba toast

In a mixer or with a wooden spoon, work 1/2 pound butter or margarine until it is soft and creamy. Crumble into small pieces 1/4 pound Roquefort or blue cheese and work until butter and cheese are well blended. Add 2 tablespoons dry sherry, 2 teaspoons finely cut chives or parsley; press the mixture into a small bowl or mold. Place in the freezing compartment of the refrigerator. Let stand at least 1 hour, or as long as you wish— the longer, the mellower.

At Serving Time:

Loosen the cheese by running a sharp knife around the edges of the bowl or mold, then turn it upside down in the center of a serving plate and give it a thump to remove. If it's balky use a thin-bladed knife to loosen. Surround cheese with toasted rye bread cut into finger lengths or whole-wheat Melba toast warmed in the oven. Provide several spreaders to scoop little hunks of frozen cheese onto the hot toast; eat without spreading.

CHEESE STRAWS

Those crusts of bread that are ordinarily thrown away make delicious salad or soup accompaniments. They may also be served with cocktails.

YOU WILL NEED:

Crusts of bread
Butter, margarine, or salad oil
Grated sharp cheese
Salt and pepper
Paprika
Caraway seeds (optional)

Arrange bread crusts on a pie pan or cookie sheet. Brush with melted butter, margarine, or salad oil. Sprinkle generously with grated sharp cheese and with salt, pepper, and paprika. A few caraway seeds may be used if desired. Set in a moderate oven, 350° F., just long enough to melt the cheese.

At Serving Time:

These are best when served warm.

GLAMORIZED HOT DOGS

The lowly little sausage is welcome at any party, especially if it's the dainty canned Vienna sausage nestled in small finger rolls.

YOU WILL NEED:

Vienna sausage
Finger rolls
Butter or margarine
1/8 teaspoon chili powder

Drain and grill sausages. Split finger rolls. Spread with butter or margarine into which you have mixed 1/8 teaspoon chili powder.

At Serving Time:

Serve piping hot. If you want to make them ahead of time, wrap in foil, freeze, and reheat—still in the foil—in oven or under broiler.

COCKTAIL CABBAGE AFLAME—WITH SHRIMP

If your party falls on Friday, or if you would like to have a dramatic cocktail table, try this.

YOU WILL NEED:

1 red cabbage
2 pounds cooked shrimp
Olive oil
Lemon or lime juice or vinegar

Salt and pepper to taste
1 clove garlic, crushed
1/2 teaspoon curry powder
1 cup sour cream

Choose the prettiest cabbage you can find, preferably one with large, loose outer leaves. Cut the stem end so that the cabbage will sit firmly on the platter or plate. Turn back the outside leaves like the petals of a great rose. With a very sharp knife, scoop a round hole out of the top of the cabbage just large enough to hold a can of Sterno.

Drain canned or quick-frozen cooked shrimp. If the black line around the edge of the shrimp has not been removed, take it out with a sharp paring knife. Cover the shrimp with French dressing made by combining 4 parts olive oil with 1 part lemon or lime juice, or vinegar; season with plenty of salt and pepper, add 1 clove garlic thoroughly crushed. Let shrimp stand, covered by the French dressing, for several hours or overnight. Prepare a dipping sauce by adding 1/2 teaspoon curry powder to 1 cup sour cream.

At Serving Time:

Drain shrimp, spear with toothpicks, and stud the cabbage with the shrimp. Light the Sterno and allow guests to heat the shrimp over the flame. Some like the shrimp cold, some like it hot. Everybody will enjoy the curried sour-cream sauce.

QUICK CRABMEAT LORENZO

Canned or quick-frozen cooked crabmeat with undiluted cream of mushroom soup makes a quick and easy version of one of the world's most famous canapés.

YOU WILL NEED:

1 cup cooked crabmeat
4 or 5 tablespoons condensed cream of
   mushroom soup
Cayenne
1 teaspoon lemon juice or dry sherry
Melba toast
Melted butter or margarine
Grated cheese

Flake and separate 1 cup cooked crabmeat. If there are any large hunks, crumble them. Remove gristle. Moisten with 4 or 5 tablespoons condensed cream of mushroom soup, dipping the soup right out of the can without diluting it. The mixture should be quite thick—thick enough to drop in blobs from a teaspoon. Season with a few grains cayenne pepper and 1 teaspoon lemon juice or dry sherry. Brush 1½-inch pieces of Melba toast with melted butter or margarine; pile mixture on toast, sprinkle with grated cheese, and set in a hot oven, 375° F., just long enough to brown, about 5 minutes.

MAKES 20.

At Serving Time:

Pass the canapés as soon as they are out of the oven. If the browning is done on a heatproof platter that can go from oven to table, all the better!

MELON WITH PROSCIUTTO

A traditional Italian specialty is adapted to make a modern cocktail snack.

YOU WILL NEED:

Honeydew melon, cantaloupe,
   mangos, papayas, pears, peaches, or
   apples
Italian smoked ham (prosciutto), or
   Westphalian or Smithfield ham in
   paper-thin slices

Scoop the meat of a honeydew melon (or whichever fruit you choose) into balls or cut the melon into squares. Wrap each piece in a strip of ham and secure with a toothpick. Remove some of the ham fat if you think there is too much.

At Serving Time:

Arrange the ham-wrapped morsels on a large attractive plate; decorate with leaves and flowers if you have them. Provide a pepper grinder or two so that each guest can add a grind of fresh black pepper to the melon before he plops it into his mouth. This appetizer is particularly good with sherry.

TURKISH SPICED MUSHROOMS

This Near East specialty is made with canned whole mushrooms.

YOU WILL NEED:

2 (3-ounce) cans whole mushrooms
Spiced vinegar from a jar of pickles
   (sweet or sour), or 2/3 cup vinegar, 1/2
   cup water, 1 onion, and 1 tablespoon
   pickling spices

Drain the liquid from 2 (3-ounce) cans whole mushrooms. Heat the liquid left from a jar of pickles. You may make your own pickling vinegar by simmering together for about 5 minutes ²/₃ cup vinegar, ¹/₂ cup water, 1 small thinly sliced onion, and 1 tablespoon mixed pickling spices. (This makes enough liquid to cover 2 [3-ounce] cans mushrooms.) Pour the hot spiced liquid over the mushrooms, cool, and set in refrigerator for several hours or preferably overnight.

At Serving Time:

Simply bring the bowl of mushrooms to the table, provide toothpicks, and let the guests spear the mushrooms from the spiced liquid. Or, drain and arrange on a relish tray along with other tidbits.

CUCUMBER CANAPÉS

Almost any spread for bread or a cracker will take on a special zest when piled on top of a crisp cucumber slice. Unless the cucumber has a tough skin it's better not to peel it. It looks prettier and the slice has more body.

YOU WILL NEED:

1 tender young cucumber
Cream cheese or cottage cheese
Horseradish or Worcestershire sauce
Paprika
Chopped chives, parsley, or finely
    chopped sweet red peppers

Cut the cucumber in slices about ¹/₄-inch thick. Since cucumbers become limp on standing, it is best not to slice them too far ahead of time. Top each slice with a cocktail spread of creamed cottage cheese mixed with chopped chives or parsley, or cream cheese seasoned with horseradish or Worcestershire sauce.

At Serving Time:

Arrange on a plate and sprinkle with paprika, chopped chives, chopped parsley, or finely chopped sweet red peppers.

MEXICAN GUACAMOLE

From Mexico originally came the idea for this creamy, unusual, and delicious spread.

YOU WILL NEED:

1 avocado
1 small tomato, diced
1/4 cup chili sauce
2 tablespoons finely chopped onion
1 tablespoon chopped green pepper or
   pimiento
French dressing
Finely chopped parsley or chives

With a silver knife, cut the avocado in half lengthwise. Remove seed. Scoop the flesh carefully from its shell. Save the shell. With a silver fork mash the pulp, then mix in thoroughly 1 diced tomato, 1/4 cup chili sauce, 2 tablespoons finely chopped onion, 1 tablespoon chopped green pepper or pimiento.

Moisten with French dressing made with 2 parts olive oil and 1 part lime or lemon juice or wine vinegar, and plenty of salt. Put the mixture back into the avocado shell and sprinkle the top with finely chopped parsley or chives.

At Serving Time:

Place the guacamole in the shell in the center of a plate. Surround with potato chips, celery sticks, carrot sticks, Melba toast, or tortillas (these come in cans). Provide spreaders for your guests to serve themselves.

BRANDIED LIVER TERRINE

This tastes for all the world like one of the homemade pâtés of France.

YOU WILL NEED:

1 (3-ounce) can liver pâté
6 tablespoons butter or margarine
1 (3-ounce) can mushrooms, chopped
1 tablespoon brandy
Finely cut parsley or chives

Use equal quantities canned liver pâté and butter or margarine: a 3-ounce can of liver pâté and 3 ounces, or 6 tablespoons butter or margarine. Melt the butter in a frying pan and gently brown a 3-ounce can of chopped mushrooms, well drained. Add the liver pâté to the butter and mushrooms and season with 1 tablespoon good brandy or cognac. Mix well and place the mixture in a small but pretty crock. Smooth the top and cover with a generous layer of parsley or chives, finely cut with scissors. Set in the refrigerator for several hours or overnight to blend the flavors.

At Serving Time:

Place the crock in the center of a decorative plate or small platter. Surround with Melba toast rounds, thinly sliced pumpernickel cut into squares, crisp French rolls cut into ½-inch slices, or bread sticks. Provide several butter spreaders and let the guests spread their own.

MONTE BENITO

A most interesting canapé, this is a miniature version of the Monte Cristo and Monte Carlo sandwiches of San Francisco that have achieved great popularity for lunches and suppers—double-deckers and all. A Monte Cristo is made with sliced chicken or turkey and sliced cheese—Monterey jack, Swiss, or Cheddar. Monte Carlo has a layer of tongue or ham along with cheese.

YOU WILL NEED:

Frozen French toast
Chicken, turkey, cheese, ham, etc.,
   sliced
Butter or margarine

Between slices of frozen French toast place any 2 of the sandwich fillings or use sliced cheese of any variety. Cut into halves for an entrée or bite-bits for an appetizer. Bake as directed on package and brush with softened butter or margarine before serving.

Variation:

Blue Benitos

Follow directions above but fill with blue cheese.

BLINI

A package of buckwheat-pancake mix or any other good pancake mix will make delicate and authentic-tasting blini, perfect to serve with diced, smoked salmon, red or black caviar, and sour cream for a Sunday luncheon. Made small, they are the most elegant overtures to dinner.

YOU WILL NEED:

1 cup buckwheat pancake mix
1 cup sour milk, buttermilk, or yogurt
1 tablespoon butter or margarine
1 egg, separated
Sour cream
Chopped onions or chives
Red and black caviar

In a blender or mixing bowl place 1 cup buckwheat pancake mix, 1 cup sour milk, buttermilk, or yogurt, 1 tablespoon butter or margarine, 1 egg yolk. Blend 30 seconds. Leave uncovered at room temperature until ready to use. Fold in 1 stiffly beaten egg white.

Drop batter by tablespoonfuls onto a well-greased griddle preheated to 380° F. As soon as the cake begins to look dry and is pocked with tiny air holes, turn with a spatula and cook briefly on the other side. Never turn a blini or pancake more than once or it will lose its delicate tenderness. As pancakes are finished, place them on a preheated hot tray. Do not stack. Do not cover.

MAKES ABOUT 3 DOZEN DOLLAR-SIZE BLINI.

At Serving Time:

Brush with melted butter or margarine and serve on heated plates. Have on hand in little bowls sour cream, chopped onions or chives, and red or black caviar. Each person puts on his blini a dab of caviar and sour cream and/or onion or chives if desired.

RAW VEGETABLE HORS D'OEUVRES

These are a boon to all who must watch their calories or their diets. Hors d'oeuvres made of raw vegetables can be a joy to the epicure, and a treat to the eyes as well as the palate. Only the freshest and most perfect vegetables should be used. They should always be crisp, cold, and arranged with an eye to color and design.

For many years a famous New York restaurant has made a specialty of serving raw vegetables in a shiny black bowl filled with crushed ice. A bouquet of celery and fennel is set in the center of the ice; radishes, carrot sticks, black and green olives are set on top of the ice, covering it completely. It is an idea worth copying.

STUFFED EGGS DIAVOLO

Prepared yellow mustard takes the place of half a dozen seasonings and spices. This is a very simple deviled-egg recipe, and very good.

YOU WILL NEED:

6 hard-cooked eggs
6 teaspoons prepared yellow mustard
Salt and pepper to taste
Chopped fresh parsley or mixed fresh
   herbs
Olives or pimientos

Cut 6 hard-cooked eggs in half, lengthwise. Remove the yolks and put the whites aside in pairs. Mash yolks with a fork; add to each egg yolk 1 teaspoon prepared yellow mustard, and salt and pepper, if needed. Refill whites with the mixture.

SERVES 6 AS FIRST COURSE, MAKES 12 APPETIZERS.

At Serving Time:

Put each pair together to look like a whole egg and roll in freshly chopped parsley or a mixture of fresh herbs. Or form the seasoned yolks into little balls. Set a ball inside each egg white and garnish with parsley, sliced olives, or pimiento strips.

INTERNATIONAL CHEESE BOARD

The easiest, most talked-about party I ever gave featured cheeses of many lands set on a cheese board and platters, decorated with green leaves and tiny flags of the countries in which the various cheeses originated. Even in a middle-sized town, you will find cheeses from a number of different countries in delicatessens, large markets, or department stores with a food department, or you can order them shipped to you by mail.

YOU WILL NEED:

A selection of cheeses
Various breads and crackers
Flags of various countries

An international cheese board—like any cheese board—should include cheeses of contrasting colors, flavors, textures—for instance, creamy white cheese, yellow cheeses, hard and soft cheeses, mellow and sharp cheeses.

> From France: Brie; Camembert; and the more unusual Fromage de Foin (cheese of hay), which is actually ripened in freshly cut hay and retains that wonderful new-mown hay fragrance; Coulommiers, rather like Brie, soft, mellow, and easy to spread.
>
> From Italy: Gorgonzola, Bel Paese, Melfino, and Provolone.
>
> From Sweden: Kümmel, flecked with caraway; Crème Chantilly; Bandost.
>
> From Norway: the famous Gjetost, a dark-brown goat cheese, made with malt; Nokkelost, a Gouda type, studded surprisingly with whole cloves.
>
> From Denmark: Danish Bleu and Tilsiter.
>
> From Turkey: Kajmak, soft and mellow; and Kasher Penner, a hard white cheese.
>
> From Holland: Edam; Gouda; and Geheimrath, semihard, of a deep, golden-yellow color.
>
> From Greece: Pheta, often spelled Feta, a snowy-white cheese with the salt flavor of the brine in which it is packed.
>
> From Portugal: Saloi, which comes from Lisbon, a type of hard cheese.
>
> From Brazil: pepper cheese.
>
> From England: Cheddar and Stilton.
>
> And don't forget the famous American sharp Cheddar cheese!

At Serving Time:

Arrange the cheeses on a board or platters—a pastry board will do very well, especially if you cover it with huckleberry leaves, being sure to leave space around the cheese for cutting. Set the appropriate flag in each piece of cheese; and if the cheeses are quite unusual, you might take a moment to write out a card and set it beside the cheese. Be sure to have on hand plenty of knives and spreaders. Provide two or three baskets or plates of breadstuffs. Particularly good with cheeses are: thin black pumpernickel cut into 2-inch squares; crusty French rolls, cut into 1/2-inch slices; bread sticks, broken into 3-inch pieces; lightly toasted water biscuits; plain, crisp crackers; Melba toast. Bread or crackers should not be too highly or definitely seasoned, but should rather provide a background for the flavors of the cheeses.

EGGPLANT CAVIAR

A superlatively delicious way to prepare eggplant, this seems to turn the vegetable into an entirely different species and is always a great success with my guests. It used to be quite a lot of work to grill the eggplants, scrape out the pulp and pound it, but is much simpler if you use your electric blender.

YOU WILL NEED:

2 large or 3 medium eggplants
Lemon juice
Olive oil
1 teaspoon salt
1/4 teaspoon pepper
Dash of lemon and /or onion juice (if
    desired)
Hard-cooked eggs

Cut 2 large or 3 medium eggplants in half lengthwise. Remove pulp from 2 of the most beautiful halves, leaving shells 1/2 inch thick. Brush shells immediately with lemon juice to prevent discoloring. Slice both peeled and unpeeled eggplant about 1 inch thick. Boil until soft about 8 minutes. Cut into 1-inch cubes.

Blend 2 cups at a time with 1/2 cup light olive oil about 10 seconds. Season with 1 teaspoon salt, 1/4 teaspoon black pepper; dash of lemon or onion juice if desired. Repeat.

SERVES ABOUT 12.

At Serving Time:

Chill very well. Pile into hollowed eggplant shells, lined, if you like, with gresh grape leaves. Instead of quartered eggs, you might use chopped eggs as a garnish—whites and yolks separate —or you could use sliced eggs. Iced caviar of eggplant keeps for days in the refrigerator, but don't leave the eggs on it. Add them just before serving or the eggplant will turn them a disagreeable green.

Pass any of the classic caviar accompaniments, such as quartered lemon. Finely chopped onion or sour cream is very good. This particular version of eggplant caviar really does look and taste remarkably like the fabulous beige caviar, so much prized in the Near East.

Soup: For All Reasons

Ever since Esau sold his birthright to his brother Jacob for a bowl of savory pottage, which was undoubtedly lentil soup, soup has been one of the mainstays of good eating.

Canned or dry-mix soups are probably the most popular and among the finest of ready-to-serve foods. According to many surveys, a can of soup is America's favorite hot dish for lunch. At the evening meal, it is not only the introduction but often the main course—a most satisfying main course, too, when the soup is hearty and served over or with toast, crackers, or rice.

Moreover, a fine, thick soup or chowder, served dramatically from a tureen, bowl, casserole, or chafing dish, becomes the pièce de résistance for informal company meals, or even on the buffet. After years of sampling canned soup in all price ranges, it is a joy to be able to report that the most readily available popular-priced brands are usually the best. Since they are intended to appeal to millions of people, they cannot be distinctively seasoned. But this allows plenty of leeway for your imagination.

Always correct the seasoning after the soup has been heated, or just before it goes to the table if it's a cold soup, because heating or mellowing brings out certain flavors, suppresses others. When using herbs or spices, don't be too lavish at first—you can always add more! A quarter of a teaspoon of dried herbs should be enough to impart a subtle flavoring to a can of soup (about 20 ounces). It's a pretty good rule of thumb to use three times as much fresh herb as dried.

In many of these recipes, wine has been substituted for part of the required milk or water. Here again, you may step up the proportion of wine, but be sure to taste as you go. You don't want your soup to taste like an alcoholic beverage!

The manner in which you serve soup is important. In most cases we have suggested that you bring it to the table in a tureen or casserole and ladle the hot soup into heated soup plates or bowls. This is no mere conceit. There is all the difference in the world between a really hot, hot soup and one that is wanly luke-warm. To heat plates or bowls, place them in the warming oven or a heated and turned-off regular oven, where the temperature is about 150°F. This amount of heat will not harm even the finest china.

In many cases we have suggested that garnishes be added to the soup as it is served at the table. Sometimes a small decanter of wine is passed so it may be added according to individual fancy.

BROCCOLI SOUP PARMENTIER

Parmentier always means there are potatoes here!

YOU WILL NEED:

1 (10³/₄-ounce) can condensed cream
   of potato soup
1¹/₂ soup-cans milk
¹/₂ (10-ounce) package frozen cut
   broccoli
Dash nutmeg
Dash pepper

Heat together 1 can condensed cream of potato soup, 1¹/₂ soup-cans milk, ¹/₂ (10-ounce) package frozen cut broccoli. Add a dash nutmeg and a dash pepper.

SERVES 4.

CREAM OF CLAM SOUP

YOU WILL NEED:

1 (7½-ounce) can minced clams
1 cup chicken stock
½ cup heavy cream
Chopped parsley

Blend 1 (7½-ounce) can minced clams with 1 cup chicken stock and ½ cup heavy cream. Heat but do not boil, and serve.

SERVES 4.

At Serving Time:

Garnish with chopped parsley.

MAKE-BELIEVE SORREL SOUP

Always in France, and sometimes in New York and San Francisco, you will find sorrel in the market; some call it sour grass, others call it schav. It makes one of the world's most interesting chilled soups. In the Virgin Islands we discovered a way to produce the soup with frozen chopped spinach and sour salt. Lemon juice or vinegar may be used instead.

YOU WILL NEED:

1 package frozen chopped spinach
¼ cup chopped onion
1 teaspoon salt
¼ teaspoon freshly ground black
   pepper
1 teaspoon (4 to 6 crystals) sour salt or
   1 to 2 tablespoons lemon juice or
   vinegar
2 eggs
4 tablespoons commercial sour cream
Hard-cooked eggs or small whole
   cooked potatoes
Chives

To 1 package frozen chopped spinach add 5 cups boiling water, 1/4 cup chopped onion, 1 teaspoon salt, 1/4 teaspoon freshly ground black pepper, and 1 teaspoon sour salt (4 to 6 crystals) or 1 to 2 tablespoons lemon juice or vinegar. (Sour salt or citric acid is available in almost any supermarket or drugstore.) Bring to a boil, cover, lower heat, and cook slowly about 10 minutes. Place in freezer 5 minutes. Meanwhile, beat 2 eggs with 2 tablespoons cold water until very light, gradually adding a little of the soup to the eggs. Then turn the eggs into the spinach soup. Put back into freezer to chill thoroughly. Ten minutes should do it.

SERVES 4 TO 6.

At Serving Time:

Stir in 4 tablespoons sour cream. Serve in chilled soup plates with sliced or diced hard-cooked eggs and/or a small whole cooked potato. Add a sprinkle of chives!

BROWN POTATO SOUP

YOU WILL NEED:

1 (10³/₄-ounce) can condensed cream
  of potato soup
10 ounces brown stock, consommé, or
  ham stock
Croutons made with toasted brown
  bread

Prepare cream of potato soup, but instead of using milk or cream, dilute with rich brown stock or canned consommé. Ham stock may also be used.

SERVES 2.

At Serving Time:

Garnish with croutons of toasted brown bread.

GAZPACHO

A perfect summer soup.

YOU WILL NEED:

4 ripe tomatoes, skinned and
   quartered
½ large green pepper, seeded and
   sliced
½ onion, sliced
1 cucumber, peeled and sliced
1 clove garlic
1 teaspoon salt
¼ teaspoon freshly ground black
   pepper
2 tablespoons olive oil
3 tablespoons wine vinegar

Skin and quarter 4 ripe tomatoes, seed and slice ½ large green pepper, peel and slice ½ small onion and 1 cucumber, and place in blender. Add 1 clove garlic, 1 teaspoon salt, ¼ teaspoon freshly ground black pepper, 2 tablespoons olive oil, 3 tablespoons wine vinegar, and ½ cup ice water. Cover and blend just 2 seconds. Chill in refrigerator.

SERVES 6.

At Serving Time:

Pour into serving plates and serve with an ice cube in the center of each plate.

ONION SOUP WITH CLARET

Canned or dehydrated onion soups can be given great distinction by the addition of claret, Burgundy, or sherry.

YOU WILL NEED:

1 can, or 1 package dehydrated, onion
   soup
½ cup claret or Burgundy, or ¼ cup
   sherry
French bread
Garlic bread
Grated Parmesan, Gruyère, or
   Romano cheese

For dehydrated onion soup follow the package directions, but substitute for part of the water ½ cup claret or Burgundy or ¼ cup sherry. The same amount of wine may be added to canned, ready-to-serve onion soup. The soup should not be allowed to boil vigorously after the wine is added.

SERVES 2 TO 4.

At Serving Time:

Serve in individual casseroles or one large casserole. Top with crusts of garlic bread made by rubbing inch-thick slices of French bread with a cut clove or garlic, brushing with melted butter or olive oil, and browning in the oven or under the broiler.

    There are two ways of serving onion soup. One school insists that the bread crusts be placed on the soup, sprinkled thickly with grated cheese, and set in a hot oven till the cheese melts and browns slightly, about 5 minutes. Others prefer to dip the soup onto the plates over the toast and pass freshly grated Parmesan, Gruyère, or Romano cheese.

VICHYSSOISE I

Several varieties of canned vichyssoise are quite good, but all need a certain amount of dressing up.

YOU WILL NEED:

1 (10³/4-ounce) can vichyssoise
1/2 cup heavy cream or sour cream
Chives
Freshly ground black pepper

Follow the directions on the can for preparation of vichyssoise. Some types of vichyssoise are condensed and require the addition of milk or cream, others are ready to serve. Chill very well. To save time, place in the freezing compartment of the refrigerator.

SERVES 2 TO 4.

At Serving Time:

Stir into the chilled soup 1/2 cup heavy cream or sour cream. Serve in ice-cold cups, garnish with plenty of chopped chives, and pass the pepper grinder.

VICHYSSOISE II

The simplest of ingredients available at any corner store make up this version of the glamorous vichyssoise.

YOU WILL NEED:

2 cups mashed potatoes
1 tablespoon butter
1 (10³/4-ounce) can condensed cream
   of chicken soup
1 teaspoon onion salt
1 cup light cream or 1 1/2 cups milk
Finely cut green onion tops or
   chopped chives.

To 2 cups fluffy-smooth mashed potatoes add 1 tablespoon butter, 1 can condensed cream of chicken soup, and 1 teaspoon onion salt, and beat well. Add 1 cup light cream or 1^1/$_2$ cups milk. Chill.

SERVES 2 TO 4.

At Serving time:

Serve in cold soup cups or glass bowls set in crushed ice, if possible. Garnish the ice with green leaves. Garnish each portion with finely cut green onion tops or chopped chives.

LOBSTER BISQUE DELUXE

This bisque of lobster has a heavenly rosy color, a heady aroma, and the flavor of wine.

YOU WILL NEED:

1 (10^3/$_4$-ounce) can cream of chicken
   soup
1 soup-can milk or milk and cream
1 cup cooked lobster meat
1 teaspoon sweet Hungarian paprika
2 tablespoons sherry
^{1}/$_4$ teaspoon nutmeg (optional)
Cayenne
Parsley, watercress, or green pepper
   rings

Heat to boiling point 1 can cream of chicken soup and 1 soup-can milk or ^{1}/$_2$ milk and ^{1}/$_2$ cream. Add 1 cup cooked lobster meat cut in small pieces, 1 teaspoon sweet Hungarian paprika for color and delicious flavor, 2 tablespoons sherry, ^{1}/$_4$ teaspoon nutmeg, and a few grains cayenne pepper.

SERVES 2 TO 4.

At Serving Time:

Bring to the table in a bowl or tureen, ladle into heated soup plates or bowls, and garnish with chopped parsley or watercress, or green pepper rings.

STURBRIDGE VILLAGE CORN CHOWDER

This old-time corn chowder is still served at the Levi Lincoln House in Sturbridge Village. When you can't think of a thing you want to eat for lunch or supper, this modern version of an old-time favorite will surely tempt you. Modern households are more likely to have bacon on hand than the salt pork called for in older recipes, so we've used bacon.

YOU WILL NEED:

6 slices bacon
1 onion
2 cups boiled, sliced potatoes
1 (15-ounce) can cream-style corn
4 cups milk
Salt and pepper to taste
Worcestershire sauce
2 tablespoons butter
Paprika
Parsley
Crackers

With a pair of scissors or sharp knife cut 6 slices of bacon into small pieces and fry. Leave bacon bits and fat in the pan, adding to it 1 medium-sized onion, thinly sliced. Cook 5 minutes over a low flame, stirring often so that the onion does not burn. Add 2 cups boiled, sliced potatoes (cut ¼ inch thick); 2 cups boiling water; 1 can cream-style corn; 4 cups milk. Heat to boiling point; season with salt, pepper, and a little Worcestershire sauce.

SERVES 6 TO 8.

At Serving Time:

Pour into a heated tureen or casserole; add 2 tablespoons butter and a sprinkling of paprika and/or parsley. Place a cracker (Saltine type) in the bottom of a bowl or a soup plate, ladle chowder over the cracker. This makes a generous amount of chowder.

MANHATTAN CLAM CHOWDER

Most popular brands of canned clam chowder are made with tomato rather than milk. Hence, by definition, they are Manhattan clam chowder. A garnish of green pepper rings, onion rings, and caraway seeds adds distinction to them.

YOU WILL NEED:

1 (10³/₄-ounce) can Manhattan-style
   clam chowder
1 tablespoon bacon fat or butter
   (optional)
1 green pepper, cut in rings
1 onion, sliced in rings
Caraway seeds

Add 1 can water to 1 can condensed Manhattan-style clam chowder. If a richer flavor is desired, 1 tablespoon bacon fat or butter may be added. Bring to a boil and simmer a few minutes.

SERVES 2 TO 4.

At Serving Time:

Ladle into heated bowls or soup plates and garnish with green pepper rings, thinly sliced onion rings, and/or a scatter of caraway seeds.

NEW ENGLAND CLAM CHOWDER

When milk is used in place of tomato, the chowder becomes New England-style and is much admired Down East. White table wine may be substituted for part of the milk.

YOU WILL NEED:

1 (10³/₄) can condensed New
   England-style clam chowder
1 soup-can milk or ¹/₂ can milk and
   ¹/₂ can dry white wine
Pilot crackers
Paprika, chopped chives, or parsley

To 1 (10³/₄-ounce) can condensed New England-style clam chowder add 1 soup-can milk or ¹/₂ can milk and ¹/₂ can dry white wine. Heat but do not boil.

SERVES 2 TO 4.

At Serving Time:

Place a pilot cracker in the bottom of a heated bowl or soup plate, ladle the chowder over the cracker, and sprinkle with paprika, chopped chives, or parsley.

CHICKEN AND WATERCRESS SOUP, MANDARIN-STYLE

A can, or package of dehydrated, chicken noodle soup combines with fresh watercress to make a soup with Oriental overtones.

YOU WILL NEED:

1 can chicken noodle soup or 1
   package dehydrated chicken noodle
   soup
1 tablespoon butter or margarine, or 1
   chicken bouillon cube
1 cup watercress
1 hard-cooked egg, sliced or quartered

Make canned chicken noodle soup or dehydrated chicken noodle soup according to package directions. Simmer to blend all flavors. For extra richness add 1 tablespoon butter or margarine, or 1 chicken bouillon cube. Add 1 cup (a large handful) watercress, leaves and tender sprigs, put the cover on the soup, and allow to sit in a warm place for about 1 or 2 minutes, just long enough to wilt the watercress.

SERVES 2 TO 4.

At Serving Time:

Ladle into bowls or plates and garnish, if desired, with slices or quarters of hard-cooked egg.

SMALL-TOWN BORSCHT

If your own corner store does not carry canned borscht, you can easily make up your own in a few minutes from the most ordinary ingredients.

YOU WILL NEED:

2 (10³/₄-ounce) cans consommé,
1 cup canned shredded beets (drain
 and reserve beet juice)
1 cup coarsely chopped cabbage
2 onions, sliced or coarsely chopped
2 tablespoons vinegar or lemon juice
1 teaspoon sugar
1 can boiled potatoes
Sour cream

Combine 2 cans consommé, 2 soup-cans water; add 1 cup canned, cut-up or shredded beets, 4 tablespoons beet juice, 1 cup coarsely chopped cabbage, 2 onions, sliced or coarsely chopped, 2 tablespoons vinegar or lemon juice, 1 teaspoon sugar. Cook all together until cabbage is just tender. Do not strain.

SERVES 4.

At Serving Time:

Ladle into bowls, add ¹/₂ boiled potato or a couple of canned whole Irish potatoes to each serving. Top with a large spoonful of thick sour cream.

BOUILLABAISSE

This is a simplified but delicious version of the great fish specialty of Marseilles, which has inspired poets, dazzled gourmets, delighted eaters all over the world. Every single one of the ingredients can be kept on hand on the pantry shelf or in the frozen-food compartment of your refrigerator.

YOU WILL NEED:

2 medium onions, thinly sliced
1 or 2 cloves garlic, crushed
2 leeks, sliced
1/2 cup olive oil
3 pounds quick-frozen flounder,
   whiting, sole, haddock, perch,
   whitefish, or a combination of these
1 cup canned tomatoes
1 bay leaf
1 cup canned oysters, clams, or mussels
   (optional)
1 cup canned or quick-frozen cooked
   shrimp, crab, or lobster meat, or
   rock lobster tails
1/2 cup canned pimiento, cut in pieces
1/2 teaspoon saffron
Salt and pepper
1 lemon or 1 cup white wine (optional)
French bread
1/4 cup chopped parsley

Sauté 2 medium-sized onions, thinly sliced, 1 or 2 crushed garlic cloves, and 2 sliced leeks in 1/2 cup olive oil until golden brown. (If you can't get leeks in your market, use more onion.) Thaw 3 pounds of quick-frozen fish fillets just enough to cut into serving pieces. Add pieces of fish along with 1 cup canned tomatoes, 1 bay leaf, and 2 cups water to onion mixture. Simmer about 15 minutes. Add 1 cup oysters, clams, or mussels (these may be omitted, if desired), and 1 cup shrimp, crabmeat, or lobster, 1/2 cup canned pimiento, cut into small pieces. Season with ½ teaspoon saffron, salt, pepper, and the juice of 1 lemon and/or 1 cup white wine. Heat but do not boil.

SERVES 8.

At Serving Time:

Bring to the table in a tureen or casserole. Some people pour off the broth, arrange the fish on a platter, and combine them once again in the serving dish, but this seems like too much trouble. Place a thick slice of French bread in each soup plate or bowl, spoon the bouillabaisse (fish and broth) on top of the bread, and sprinkle with chopped parsley. Served with a salad, fruit, and cheese for dessert, it's a magnificent meal.

ST. JOSEPH'S MINESTRA

This is served in Italy on St. Joseph's Day, March 19, but it's good any day of the year.

YOU WILL NEED:

1 clove garlic
1 large can (at least 10¾ ounces)
   minestrone
1 can condensed consommé.
1 package frozen spinach
Freshly grated Romano or Parmesan
   cheese
Chopped parsley

Rub a saucepan with a cut clove garlic, just as you would rub a salad bowl. Pour into saucepan 1 large can minestrone, adding water if directions call for it. Also add 1 can condensed consommé and 1 soup-can water. Bring to a boil. Add 1 package frozen leaf spinach. Cook until vegetable is just beginning to soften but still retains its character.

Sprinkle with freshly grated (or freshly opened) Romano or Parmesan cheese. Have a small bowl of chopped parsley on hand —preferably broad-leaf Italian parsley.

SERVES 4 TO 6.

At Serving Time:

Serve with plenty of crusty Italian bread or brown 'n' serve club rolls.

FRUIT SOUP

YOU WILL NEED:

2 (10-ounce) packages frozen
   raspberries
1 (6-ounce) can frozen orange juice
1 tablespoon cornstarch
1/2 pint sour cream or yogurt

Let 2 (10-ounce) packages frozen raspberries and 1 (6-ounce) can frozen orange juice stand unopened at room temperature for about 1 hour to defrost. Drain raspberries, reserving 1/2 cup of syrup. Mix 1/4 cup syrup with 1 tablespoon cornstarch. Heat remaining syrup slowly and stir in cornstarch mixture. Cook, stirring, until thick and clear. When well cooled, add orange juice and blend in 1/2 pint sour cream or yogurt and raspberries. Chill well.

SERVES 6.

At Serving Time:

Serve in chilled cups, small bowls, or sherbet glasses.

Chilled Soups and the Blender

The biggest chilled-soup news of the decade is the role of the electric blender. Amazing how it whirs together, from canned soups, within seconds, delicious prototypes of some of the world's most elaborate and time-consuming specialties with no cooking at all.

Because it does such an extraordinary job of distributing and incorporating ingredients, the blender makes it unnecessary to "mellow the soup for several hours in a cold place," as the old recipes suggest. Not only does the blender make the finest of purees, but a single minute in the blender merges the flavors as effectively as hours of standing and gives the effect of simmering.

PEACH SOUP GLACÉ CHARENTE

This chilled soup is an innovation for America. However, it probably dates back to the Polish and Russian nobility, who have had an enormous influence on French cuisine. The original recipe involves considerable doing—peeling, seeding, cutting up, stewing very lightly, and ever so carefully sweetening. Afterward, the peaches were put through a sieve, flavored, thickened with cornstarch, chilled overnight, and eventually mixed with crême fraiche *and lemon juice or sour cream.*

Our brain-wave telescopes hours into seconds—uses a can of peach-pie filling and, to save calories, cholesterol, and money . . . plain yogurt.

YOU WILL NEED:

1 (16-ounce) can peach-pie filling
2 tablespoons cognac
1/2 teaspoon cinnamon
1/4 teaspoon cloves
1 cup yogurt
1 fresh peach
Chinese noodles or croutons

In two takes, whir in electric blender 1 (16-ounce) can peach-pie filling; 4 cups ice and water; 2 tablespoons cognac; 1/2 teaspoon cinnamon; 1/4 teaspoon cloves. Stir in 1 cup yogurt.

SERVES 8.

At Serving Time:

Serve from chilled tureen into frosty cold bowls or cups. Garnish with a slice of fresh peach, if available.

Stock, Broth, and Fumet

As every cook and cookbook reader knows, hundreds, even thousands and tens of thousands of recipes call for some sort of stock—beef, veal, chicken, or mushroom or fish fumet. Certainly one can substitute canned broths and consommé. Many of these are excellent. Bouillon cubes, meat glazes, and various concentrates can also do yeoman service in the kitchen. Some have good flavor; others have no flavor other than salt.

We found that with the pressure cooker, bones and scraps of meat, dibs and dabs of almost anything could be transmuted with very little effort into rich, highly concentrated stocks, broths, bouillon, consommé, and aspic bases. Since comparatively little liquid is used, the broths come from the kettle already concentrated. No long cooking or reducing is necessary. All the meat juices, the marrow and gelatins from the bones, all the lovely glisten of homemade soup, come forth in a rush. The stock can be skimmed if you insist, but it isn't necessary. The so-called scum that rises to the top is nothing more nor less than precious protein and albumin. Although it may not look too pretty, these proteins give a right fine taste.

The miracle of broth takes place in a pressure cooker in half an hour or less. It doesn't take a day or "a day and a night" as Escoffier requires. Even if the stock were to be used immediately or within hours, it would still be worth making in the pressure cooker. But nowadays you can team your pressure cooker with another wonder worker, the freezer. Pour the stock into ice-cube trays. Next morning remove any fat that has collected on the top. Store the cubes in plastic bags; close with twisters. Tag and date them. Use the fat that has been removed for browning meats or seasoning all sorts of soups and sauces. Whenever you want stock, add one or two of your cubes to a cup of water and simmer for a few minutes.

Not since the days when our grandmothers gloated over their treasure troves of homemade jams, preserves, and jellies have there been such feelings of accomplishment and luxury as you will experience when you see in your freezer plastic bags filled with frozen cubes of your own gourmet stock. Craig Claiborne, food editor of *The New York Times*, makes it clear that if anyone cares to give him a present, he would like, please, some frozen cubes of concentrated fish fumet. Something different, certainly, in the way of a gourmet gift!

Making Your Own Stocks

These homemade stocks made in the pressure cooker have a richness and depth of flavor impossible to achieve in any of the soups or stocks commercially available. If you want to use them for cooking, they need not be skimmed or cleared. The so-called scum that rises to the top contains valuable and delicious proteins and albumins. The recipes given here are highly concentrated and very lightly seasoned. You will notice that we are chary about using herbs, for if the stocks are to be frozen into cubes and kept in bags, you may discover that herbs change flavor, developing slightly off-tastes.

The strength of your homemade stock will necessarily vary according to the materials on hand. Generally you will find that 2 of your own ice-cube-size blocks can be diluted with 1 cup of water. For the best taste add the cubes to cold water, bring to a boil, simmer 2 or 3 minutes, then season to taste.

Choosing Meats for Stock

The best choice of meat is a middle cut of beef shin or brisket. However, many other soup meats will do. The bones must be cracked. Better ask for two-thirds lean meat and one-third bone and fat.

Add to the stock pot any bones or bits of cooked meats—cooked beef or veal chops or bones from roast beef or fowl. Your choice is almost limitless. For an all-purpose stock, smoked or corned meats are not used nor are lamb or mutton because each has such a distinctive flavor of its own.

BROWN STOCK

One of the basics of fine cooking, this recipe gives you a highly concentrated broth almost like what the French chefs call a demiglaze. We suggest browning the meat so that the stock will have a deep-brown color and added richness of flavor. However, you can get by without browning the meat, although the flavor will be a little different. The color can be deepened by adding a few drops of Kitchen Bouquet or Gravymaster.

YOU WILL NEED:

4 pounds shin of beef and bones,
   including marrow bones if possible
4 cups water or to cover
1 teaspoon salt
1 small onion stuffed with 3 cloves
1 sprig parsley
1/4 cup chopped celery leaves or 1
   teaspoon dried celery flakes
1/2 bay leaf
1 carrot, sliced
Pepper to taste

Remove lean meat from 4 pounds shin bones of beef and cut into 1-inch cubes. Brown the cubes in 3 tablespoons melted suet or marrow from the bones. This can be done in the pressure cooker kettle, which should in this case be set at high heat, close to 400°. Add more marrow if needed. Put fat, bones, and remaining meat cubes into the kettle. Cover with cold water, using 1 cup water to each pound meat. Add 1 teaspoon salt. Cooker should never be more than ⅔ full. Add 1 small onion stuffed with 3 cloves, a sprig parsley, ¼ cup chopped celery leaves or 1 teaspoon dried celery flakes, ½ bay leaf, and 1 carrot, sliced. Allow to stand 1 hour at room temperature to draw out juices. Cook under pressure 20 minutes. Let pressure go down normally so that more and more essence will be drawn from the bones. Strain, remove fat.

MAKES A LITTLE OVER A QUART OF HIGHLY CONCEN-TRATED STOCK, ABOUT 2½ QUARTS OF BROTH.

At Serving Time:

Dilute to the strength required, correct the seasonings, remove fat, and serve as a broth. Or freeze in ice trays. Keep in plastic bags in freezer to be used in innumerable recipes that require brown stock.

YOUR OWN CONSOMMÉ

This consommé has a marvelously subtle flavor because it is made of beef, veal, and chicken cooked together under pressure. A glorious mélange!

YOU WILL NEED:

2 pounds cubed lean beef
1 marrow bone
3 pounds knuckle of veal, cut in pieces
1 pound marrow bones
1 pound bones from chicken or
    chicken wings

$^1/_3$ cup diced carrot
$^1/_3$ cup diced celery
$^1/_3$ cup diced onion
2 tablespoons butter or chicken fat
1 teaspoon salt
$^1/_2$ teaspoon peppercorns
2 cloves
2 sprigs parsley
$^1/_2$ bay leaf
1 sprig marjoram and 2 sprigs thyme
  or $^1/_4$ teaspoon each dried marjoram
  and thyme if consommé is to be
  served immediately
Sherry or Madeira to taste

Have 2 pounds lean beef cut into 1-inch cubes. Brown $^1/_2$ the meat in some marrow from the marrow bones, at 400° F. Add this to the remaining beef cubes along with 3 pounds knuckle of veal cut in pieces, 1 pound marrow bones, and the carcass of a chicken broken up in small pieces or 1 pound chicken wings. Cover with enough cold water to fill the pressure cooker $^2/_3$ full. Allow to stand $^1/_2$ hour. Cook under pressure 20 minutes.

Meanwhile, cook $^1/_3$ cup each diced carrot, diced celery, and diced onion in 2 tablespoons butter or chicken fat 5 minutes in electric skillet at 370°. Add to the soup with 1 teaspoon salt, $^1/_2$ teaspoon peppercorns, 2 cloves, 2 sprigs parsley, $^1/_2$ bay leaf. If consommé is to be served immediately, add 1 sprig marjoram and 2 sprigs thyme or $^1/_4$ teaspoon each of the dried herbs. Add to the pressure-cooked stock. Simmer 1 hour at 200° F. Strain, cool quickly, remove fat, and clear the soup if desired.

SERVES 4 TO 6.

At Serving Time:

Correct the seasoning, flavor to taste with sherry or Madeira, and add whatever garnish you please. For future use, freeze in ice-cube trays.

FISH STOCK OR FISH FUMET

This broth made from fish bones and scraps will form the basis of glittering aspics or the most delectable sauces.

YOU WILL NEED:

3 pounds fish heads, bones, and scraps
1 carrot, finely chopped
1 onion, finely chopped
1 stalk celery, finely chopped
1 sprig parsley
3 peppercorns
1 clove
Bay leaf
2 tablespoons lemon juice
1 egg white (optional)
Yellow coloring, saffron, or curry
    powder (optional)

Place 3 pounds fish heads, bones, and scraps into a 4-quart pressure cooker. Add 1 cup of water for each pound of fish. Make sure that the cooker is not more than ²/₃ full. Then add 1 carrot, 1 onion, 1 stalk celery, all cut into small pieces, 1 sprig parsley, 3 peppercorns, 1 clove, a bit of bay leaf, 2 tablespoons lemon juice. Cook under 15 pounds pressure about 20 minutes. Allow pressure to go down naturally. This method will extract every bit of flavor and gelatin from bones and fish.

Strain stock. Clarify with egg white if you wish and use immediately or pour into ice-cube trays, freeze, and store the cubes in plastic bags.

To add a lovely golden glimmer to your stock or aspic, use a bit of yellow food coloring or flavor with saffron or a touch, but only a touch, of curry powder.

SERVES 4 TO 6.

Eggs—Original Convenience Food

Being in its natural state so close to perfect eating, the egg remains, as it must have been through history, the favorite recourse of those on the lookout for something good to eat—and quick! Yet despite the fact that speed is the very essence of egg cookery, it is not a paradox to insist that the basic principle of egg cookery is slow cooking at low temperatures. The difference in time between proper and dreadful egg cookery may be only a few seconds, but the difference in taste and texture is enormous.

POACHED EGGS

More people are more frightened of poaching eggs than of any other cooking process. As a result, innumerable gadgets have been invented requiring usually the most careful greasing of dinky poachers, the use of strange hoops of metal, and no mean knowledge of sleight-of-hand to extricate them from the shapes into which they have been tortured.

All sorts of additives have been suggested, turning the poaching water into something not unlike a pickling liquor—lemon juice, vinegar, salt. All are calculated to keep the whites firm. Generally these things make the whites not only firm but tough and rubbery.

A heavy skillet makes a wonderful egg poacher for anywhere from 1 to 6 or even 8 eggs, depending on size. The secret of this absolutely failproof method is a little neglect. We happened upon it by accident. While I was poaching eggs one busy day, the phone rang. The eggs were in the water. Hastily I covered the eggs, turned off the heat, and talked on the telephone for at least 5 minutes. The poor eggs, I thought, ruined no doubt. But no, they were perfect.

YOU WILL NEED:

Eggs (1 or 2 per serving)
Hot water

Notice that we do not add salt, pepper, seasonings, lemon juice, or vinegar. Use hot water from the tap if you wish to save time. Water should stand at least 1½ inches deep in the skillet. Bring to a boil and place eggs one at a time in the water. Push whites together with spatula so that eggs have a pretty shape. Cover. Turn heat off. Leave for at least 5 minutes or until you want to serve them.

At Serving Time:

Remove with a slotted spoon and serve on toast, fried tomato slices, or English muffins (halved and toasted), or whatever you like. Sprinkle with salt, pepper, and maybe a pinch of chives or a drop of Tabasco.

Variation:

Eggs Benedictine (some call them Benedict)

For each serving prepare 1 or 2 rounds of toasted and buttered white bread or English muffins. Top with a thin slice of cooked ham, which may be warmed in butter, if you insist. The classic way, it is actually unnecessary. Place poached eggs on top of ham and mask with hollandaise sauce, which you can buy in a jar or make in your blender with perfect ease and complete confidence. (See page 152.)

SHIRRED EGGS MORNAY

A shirred egg is an egg to remember when you are entertaining. Shirred eggs need little attention, look elegant, and are easy to serve. If you have no individual egg shirrers, heatproof glass custard cups will do very well.

YOU WILL NEED:

6 to 8 eggs
Salt and pepper to taste
1 10³/₄-ounce can undiluted
   condensed cream of chicken soup
1 slightly beaten egg
6 tablespoons grated cheese

Butter egg shirrers or individual baking dishes. Break 1 egg into each. Sprinkle with salt and pepper. Cover eggs with sauce made by adding 1 slightly beaten egg to 1 can undiluted condensed cream of chicken soup. Sprinkle each with 1 tablespoon grated cheese and bake in a moderate oven, 350° F., about 6 minutes. For easy handling it's a good idea to place the individual small dishes on a cookie sheet or broiler pan; then they can all be taken out together.

SERVES 6.

At Serving Time:

Place the shirred eggs on individual plates or arrange on a large platter and decorate the platter with bouquets of parsley or green leaves.

BUTTERED EGGS À LA ROBERT

Even for the most skillful of cooks, transferring eggs from pan to platter involves some hazard, so it's a good idea to prepare eggs in the dish in which you will serve them. A heatproof glass pie pan, for instance, can be used if you cover the heating unit or flame with an asbestos pad.

YOU WILL NEED:

3 tablespoons butter or margarine
6 eggs
Quick Robert Sauce (see pages 151-52)
Chopped fresh parsley

Melt 3 tablespoons butter or margarine in a frying pan or serving dish. Slip eggs into hot fat. Do not attempt to cook too many at once. Cook over low heat until edges show a faint line of golden brown.

SERVES 3 TO 6.

At Serving Time:

Pour Quick Robert Sauce around rather than over the eggs. Garnish with chopped fresh parsley.

SOFT, MEDIUM, OR HARD-COOKED EGGS

To keep cold eggs from cracking, run warm water over them when you take them out of the refrigerator. Prick the blunt or wide side of the egg with a safety-pin and lower into softly boiling water. Cook in just-bubbling water 2, 3, or 4 minutes depending on your taste. As soon as time is up, set pan under faucet and let cold water run into the pan to stop the cooking. Eggs may be held for some time in warm water.

Hard-cooked eggs follow same procedure as above but cook from 12 to 15 minutes.

If you don't want to bother pricking eggs, simply cover with cold water and bring to a full, rolling boil. If eggs are average size and you like a very soft cooked egg, it will be ready as soon as water comes to a big, rolling boil. You may lower heat and continue cooking 2 or 3 minutes longer. Hard-cooked eggs started in cold water should be done in 8 minutes.

CODDLED EGGS

Start eggs in cold water. Turn off heat as soon as water comes to a full boil. Cover pan. Let stand 6 to 8 minutes.

EGGS MOLLET

This is an elegant French version of eggs poached in their shells. It is one of those simple procedures which manage to terrify some of the most skilled cooks. Here again, you are practically assured of success if you prick the blunt side of the egg with a safety pin. A layer of water seems to seep in and around the egg, making it far less difficult to remove the shell neatly and smoothly.

Some chefs present their Eggs Mollet looking wavery and a little flattened like a soft poached egg. Others feel that there is more of a surprise element when the white is firm enough to hold its egg shape. A delightful contrast to the soft-gold center.

With a slotted spoon or wire sieve, lower the pricked eggs into boiling water, using about a quart of water for four eggs. Cook over medium heat, uncovered, from 4 to 6 minutes. Immediately run cold water into the pan. This sets the whites and cools the eggs so that they can be handled easily. Tap eggs all over to break shells and remove gently and carefully under running water.

Eggs Mollet are often served chilled with a mask of savory mayonnaise. Or they may be re-warmed by placing about a minute in a bowl of hot water. Drain and serve in the same manner as poached eggs.

SCRAMBLED EGGS

Every cook in the world has his own thoughts about the perfect way to scramble eggs. This is ours. Soft, tender, glistening eggs, and they require no elaborate equipment, no sleight-of-hand.

YOU WILL NEED:

4 eggs
4 tablespoons lukewarm water, salad
  oil, or sour cream
$1/4$ teaspoon white pepper
3 drops liquid hot pepper sauce
$1/2$ teaspoon lemon juice
2 tablespoons butter or margarine
$1/2$ teaspoon salt

In a small, heavy skillet slowly melt 1 tablespoon butter or margarine. Beat, but only until mixed, 4 eggs and 4 tablespoons lukewarm water, salad oil, or sour cream; or use 2 tablespoons water and 2 tablespoons salad oil. Season with $1/4$ teaspoon white pepper, 3 drops liquid hot pepper sauce, $1/2$ teaspoon lemon juice. Hold the salt ($1/2$ teaspoon) until later—it tends to toughen the eggs. Pour the seasoned eggs into the skillet and stir over moderate heat until eggs begin to set, moving constantly on and off the heat. Watch like a hawk and stop the cooking while the eggs still gleam. The heat of the pan and even that of a serving plate will continue the cooking.

SERVES 2.

At Serving Time:

To give a rich Parisian taste and shimmer, dot the eggs with another tablespoon of butter or margarine, broken into bits.

SQUIGGLED OR COUNTRY SCRAMBLED EGGS

This is a variation of scrambled eggs. Use exactly the same ingredients as above, but do not beat eggs. Simply break into the pan. Let cook about 30 seconds. Add seasonings and stir with a fork, but not too much. Little bits of unmixed white and gold should show.

FRENCH OMELET

All your life you may have heard that it takes some sort of heaven-sent power to produce a fine French omelet. You are warned that you need a special omelet pan and that this pan must never be desecrated by being used for any other purpose. The abracadabra of omelet recipes is limitless.

About all of this we quote from Porgy and Bess: *"It ain't necessarily so."*

Admirable omelets can and have been achieved in any good, heavy, well-tempered little skillet—and, though it seems a sacrilege, even upon a griddle. One secret . . . make individual omelets.

YOU WILL NEED:

2 eggs
½ teaspoon salt
¼ teaspoon pepper
1 teaspoon chopped chives and/or
   parsley (optional)
2 tablespoons warm water
1 tablespoon butter or margarine
1 tablespoon heavy or sour cream
   (optional)

Heat skillet or griddle very hot. Add 1 tablespoon butter or margarine and swirl it around. Beat until well mixed and light but not frothy 2 eggs; 2 tablespoons warm water; ½ teaspoon salt; ¼ teaspoon pepper; 1 teaspoon chopped chives and/or parsley (optional). Pour into skillet, pushing the edges together, shaking the pan. The moment the omelet starts to set, flop both ends toward the middle and turn immediately onto an unheated plate. A heated plate, obviously, would result in an overcooked omelet.

SERVES 1.

At Serving Time:

To impart a beautiful sheen, brush omelet with 1 tablespoon heavy whipping cream or sour cream.

STACKED OMELET SOUFFLÉ FLAMBÉ

As impressive as a soufflé . . . a production that dates back to the days of Madame Du Barry. Returning to her type of dairy-maid simplicity, you may make and serve in the same attractive, flameproof skillet.

Orange juice and sections may be substituted, of course.

YOU WILL NEED:

8 eggs
1/2 teaspoon salt
1/2 teaspoon lemon juice
8 tablespoons tangerine juice
4 tablespoons butter or margarine
1 (7-ounce) can mandarin orange
  sections
1/4 cup (plus a sprinkle) cognac
1/4 cup orange marmalade (the long-
  shred type)

Make 2 puffy omelets. For each one: Whip until stiff 4 egg whites, 1/4 teaspoon each salt and lemon juice. Fold in 4 egg yolks, beaten until frothy with 4 tablespoons tangerine juice. Melt 2 tablespoons butter or margarine in a heavy 10-inch pan, turning to coat sides as well as bottom. Cook slowly about 8 minutes, shaking from time to time to keep loose. Place under broiler about 2 minutes until set and gilded. Cover one omelet with well-drained mandarin orange sections (7-ounce can). Lightly sprinkle with cognac. Top with second omelet.

Suzette Sauce

Meanwhile heat together 1/4 cup each butter and marmalade (the long-shred type). Slightly warm 1/4 cup cognac, set afire. Pour both at the same time, blazing and sizzling, over the omelet.

SERVES 4 AS A MAIN DISH, 8 FOR DESSERT.

SPINACH SOUFFLÉ

At the Four Seasons restaurant in New York they serve an extraordinarily fresh-tasting and delicious spinach soufflé. Here is a quick adaptation, which tastes remarkably similar and is made from quick-frozen chopped spinach and cream of chicken soup.

YOU WILL NEED:

1 package quick-frozen chopped
   spinach
1 can condensed cream of chicken
   soup
5 eggs, separated
1/4 small onion
1/4 teaspoon nutmeg
Sour cream for garnish

Cook for only 1 minute a package of quick-frozen chopped spinach. Drain and place in the blender with 1 can condensed cream of chicken soup, 5 egg yolks, and 1/4 very small onion cut into a couple of pieces. Blend 1 minute. Pour into bowl and lightly fold in 5 stiffly beaten egg whites. Transfer to a buttered straight-sided soufflé dish about 8 inches in diameter. The dish should be filled about 7/8 full so that the soufflé will rise well above the dish. Bake at 400° F. about 30 minutes, or if you prefer a firmer soufflé, set in a pan of hot water and bake at 325° F. about 45 minutes.

SERVES 4 TO 6.

At Serving Time:

Serve immediately and pass around sour cream, which can be used as a garnishing sauce.

FRITTATA WITH GREEN BEANS

This makes a delightful main dish for lunch or supper.

YOU WILL NEED:

1 package frozen French-style green
  beans
1 tablespoon minced onion
1/2 clove garlic
2 tablespoons olive oil
4 eggs, slightly beaten
1/4 cup bread crumbs
1/4 cup tomato juice, milk, or water
1/2 teaspoon salt
1/4 teaspoon pepper

Cook a package of frozen French-style green beans according to package directions. Meanwhile, heat in a frying pan 1 tablespoon minced onion and 1/2 clove garlic in 1 tablespoon olive oil. Cook slowly until the onion is yellow. Remove garlic. Set aside. Cut beans into pieces about 1-inch long and add to 4 slightly beaten eggs along with 1/4 cup bread crumbs, which have been soaked in 1/4 cup tomato juice, milk, or water; 1/2 teaspoon salt, and 1/4 teaspoon pepper. Add remaining tablespoon of oil to the frying pan and heat. Pour in the egg-and-bean mixture, cooking slowly until the frittata is set. Place under the broiler and brown the top lightly.

SERVES 4.

At Serving Time:

Cut into 4 wedges like a pie.

The Meatless Mainstay:
Cheese, Rice, Pasta

In this chapter we have grouped a number of those dishes which, like so many great works of art, are quite unclassifiable. They are for the most part main-course dishes. Several would, with a salad and dessert, constitute one-dish meals.

Among them are such classic dishes as cheese soufflé, Swiss fondue, and a number of notable pastas. Important rice dishes are here too—pilaf and spinach rice.

There are others too, equally indispensable to anyone with an appreciation for good food.

Each one of these dishes makes use of some shortcut—a prepared sauce, a canned product, or a new technique.

PILAF INDIENNE

One of the ladies of the Indian embassy was a guest on my television show when we cooked pilaf. She asked for the recipe to give her chef at home. That's why we know that though our method is unorthodox, the flavor must be authentic.

YOU WILL NEED:

1½ cups precooked, packaged rice,
   i.e., Minute Rice
1 teaspoon salt
3 chicken bouillon cubes
¼ to ½ teaspoon curry powder
or powdered saffron

2 small onions, sliced
1/4 cup butter
1/4 cup raisins
2 tablespoons coarsely chopped salted almonds
1/4 teaspoon cinnamon
1 bay leaf
Cardamom seeds
Nutmeg
Salt and pepper
1 cup leftover chicken, lamb, beef, or ham, diced

Add to 1½ cups each precooked packaged rice and water, 1 teaspoon salt, 3 chicken bouillon cubes, and 1/4 to 1/2 teaspoon curry powder or powdered saffron. Bring to a full boil; cover and let stand in a warm place for 10 minutes.

In the meantime, fry 2 small sliced onions in 1/4 cup butter to a golden brown. Add 1/4 cup raisins, 2 tablespoons coarsely chopped salted almonds, 1/4 teaspoon cinnamon, 1 bay leaf, 2 or 3 cardamom seeds if you have them, a dash of nutmeg, salt, and freshly ground black pepper to taste. If you wish to serve this as a main dish rather than as an accompaniment, add 1 cup leftover chicken, lamb, beef, or ham, cut into small pieces. Mix with cooked rice. Heat a minute or two.
SERVES 4.

At Serving Time:

Heap on a heated platter. Garnish in the Oriental manner with chopped crisp bacon sprinkled over the top, French-fried onions (from a can), chopped chives or parsley, salted almonds, and/or sliced hard-cooked eggs.

CHEESE SOUFFLÉ

Bread is used here instead of the usual white sauce. The cheese is merely diced, not grated, and if you have a portable electric beater, you can beat the egg whites in a 2-quart straight-sided soufflé dish and merely pour on the cheese mixture.

YOU WILL NEED:

1 cup milk
3 tablespoons butter or margarine
1 slice white bread
1/2 teaspoon dry mustard
1/2 teaspoon salt
1/4 teaspoon nutmeg
1 cup diced Cheddar cheese
5 eggs

Heat 1 cup milk and 3 tablespoons butter or margarine until butter is melted. Put 1 thin slice white bread into blender with 1/2 teaspoon dry mustard, 1/2 teaspoon salt, and 1/4 teaspoon nutmeg. Cover and blend for 5 seconds. Remove cover and gradually add hot-milk mixture. With motor on add 1 cup firmly packed, diced Cheddar cheese and blend for 10 seconds. Add 5 egg yolks. Cover and blend 12 seconds. Beat 5 egg whites until stiff but not dry. Gradually pour cheese mixture over egg whites, folding the cheese into the egg whites with a rubber spatula until lightly blended. Bake in an ungreased 2-quart soufflé dish in 375° F. oven 30 to 35 minutes.

SERVES 4.

At Serving Time:

Race to the table.

QUICHE LORRAINE

One of the most famous dishes of Alsace-Lorraine is a kind of cheese custard pie, sprinkled with bits of crisp bacon. It may be made without a crust, or you can use a prepared crust.

YOU WILL NEED:

6 slices bacon
1 cup milk or light cream

1 cup grated Swiss cheese
4 eggs, slightly beaten
Onion juice or extract
1/2 teaspoon salt
1/8 teaspoon freshly ground black
   pepper
Cayenne or Tabasco
1 package plain pastry mix or a quick-
   frozen pie shell

Fry 6 slices bacon until crisp and crumble into small pieces. Mix with 1 cup milk or light cream, 1 cup grated Swiss cheese, 4 slightly beaten eggs, a few drops onion juice or extract, 1/2 teaspoon salt, 1/8 teaspoon pepper, a few grains cayenne or a couple of drops Tabasco sauce.

Line a 9-inch pie plate with plain pastry, either quick-frozen prepared or made from a packaged mix. Then pour in the cheese-and-egg mixture. Bake 10 minutes at 450° F., then reduce heat to 325° and bake until firm or when a silver knife inserted comes out clean, about 30 minutes.

SERVES 4.

At Serving Time:

Serve neither blazing hot nor cold, but gently warm. A big bowl of mixed green salad is the traditional accompaniment, and with fruit it's all you could possibly want for lunch or supper.

Variation:

Quiche Lorraine for Lent

Omit bacon and sprinkle the pie just as it comes from the oven with 1/2 cup canned French-fried onions. If you wish, you can put the onions on the custard after it is set but before it is quite ready to come out of the oven, so that the onions will be crisp and warm.

GREEN SPINACH RICE

YOU WILL NEED:

1 package frozen chopped spinach
2 cups cooked rice
1 teaspoon salt

Cook 1 package frozen chopped spinach according to directions, but only for 1 minute. Add 2 cups boiling water, 2 cups precooked rice, 1 teaspoon salt. Bring to a boil again, remove from heat, cover and let stand about 10 minutes. Fluff with a fork.

SERVES 2.

NOODLES AND GREEN PEAS

YOU WILL NEED:

2 tablespoons butter, margarine, or
  olive oil
4 slices bacon, diced
1 package frozen green peas
1/2 cup frozen chopped onion
1/2 teaspoon salt
1/2 teaspoon sugar
1/2 teaspoon meat extract
1 (8-ounce) package noodles, cooked
  according to package directions

Combine 2 tablespoons butter, margarine, or olive oil with 4 slices bacon, diced, 1 package frozen green peas, 1/2 cup frozen chopped onion, and 1 cup water. Season with 1/2 teaspoon salt, 1/2 teaspoon sugar, and 1/2 teaspoon meat extract. Bring to boil and cook about 15 minutes or until peas are soft and water almost absorbed. Toss in a bowl with an 8-ounce package of noodles cooked and drained according to directions.

SERVES 4.

MACARONI AND HAM, VIRGINIA-STYLE

A can of macaroni and cream sauce with cheese is the beginning of great wisdom for the hostess in a hurry. Merely sprinkled with cheese and heated in the oven, it is excellent. Dressed up in the manner of old Virginia, it's superb.

YOU WILL NEED:

Butter or margarine
2 cans macaroni in cream sauce with
   cheese
1 or 2 cups diced cooked ham
2 teaspoons prepared yellow mustard
   (optional)
½ cup grated Cheddar cheese
4 tablespoons bread crumbs (optional)
Parsley or watercress

Butter a baking dish. Combine 2 cans macaroni and cream sauce (yes, it comes canned with its own sauce) and 1 to 2 cups diced cooked ham. Season with 2 teaspoons prepared yellow mustard. Place in the buttered baking dish. Sprinkle with ½ cup grated cheese, and if desired, 4 tablespoons bread crumbs. Bake at 400° F. about 25 minutes or until top is brown.

SERVES 6.

At Serving Time:

Set parsley or watercress in the center of the casserole. Serve on hot plates.

GREEN NOODLES WITH MEAT SAUCE

*Green noodles are nothing more than noodles colored with spinach juice.
Since the coloring is done by the manufacturer, and the noodles are
almost as easy to procure as any other type, it's amazing what a sensation
they created when they first appeared in the U.S.A.*

YOU WILL NEED:

2 cups cooked green noodles
Prepared spaghetti sauce with or
   without meat
Basil, oregano, Worcestershire sauce,
   or red wine
1 clove garlic
Chopped parsley (optional)
Grated Parmesan or Romano cheese

Cook 2 cups green noodles according to package directions. Be
careful not to overcook. Noodles, like spaghetti, should be
cooked al dente, as the Italians say—just to the point where they
are tender but still provide something for the teeth. Drain in a
strainer and rinse with hot or cold water to separate the strands.

   Meanwhile, heat prepared spaghetti sauce. Perk it up by
adding a little extra seasoning, basil or oregano or a dash of
Worcestershire sauce or a couple of tablespoons of red table
wine such as Chianti or Burgundy.

SERVES 4.

At Serving Time:

Heat a serving dish, rub with 1 cut clove garlic, holding the clove
with a bit of waxed paper. Pile the drained noodles on the hot
plate; make a well in the center, and pour the sauce into the well.
Sprinkle, if desired, with fresh chopped parsley. Provide a bowl
of grated Parmesan or Romano cheese. Crusty bread, green
noodles, a green salad, red wine, and a fruit dessert comprise a
glorious meal.

RAVIOLI GRATINÉ

Ravioli, beloved of the Italians, are nothing more or less than square noodles filled with savory meat, chicken, vegetables, or cheese. When homemade, they take hours. But you can buy them complete with tomato sauce in a jar. In most cases the sauce can take a little doctoring, so ready-to-serve ravioli sprinkled with grated cheese and freshly chopped parsley, heated in a shallow casserole, make a good and filling dish.

YOU WILL NEED:

1 tablespoon olive oil
1 (8-ounce) can ravioli
1/4 cup chopped parsley, chives, or
   scallion tops
1/4 cup grated Parmesan or Romano
  · cheese

Pour 1 tablespoon olive oil into a shallow ovenware casserole or heatproof glass pie pan. Add ravioli with sauce. Sprinkle generously with grated Parmesan or Romano cheese. Set in a 350°F. oven, for about 20 minutes or until the ravioli are bubbly hot, the cheese melted and delicately brown.

SERVES 2.

At Serving Time:
Sprinkle with chopped parsley, chives, or scallion tops.

COTTAGE CHEESE MOLD

YOU WILL NEED:

1 envelope unflavored gelatin
1/2 teaspoon salt
1/2 cup hot water
2 cups cottage cheese
1 tablespoon prepared horseradish
1 cup heavy cream
2 cups diced cucumber
1/2 cup diced green pepper
1/4 cup sliced green onions

Put 1 envelope unflavored gelatin, 1/2 teaspoon salt, and 1/2 cup very hot water in the blender. Cover and blend at high speed for 40 seconds. Add 2 cups cottage cheese and 1 tablespoon prepared horseradish. Cover and turn motor on high. Remove cover, and with motor on, gradually pour in 1 cup heavy cream. Turn off motor and pour mixture over 2 cups diced cucumber, 1/2 cup diced green pepper, and 1/4 cup sliced green onion, and chill until firm.

SERVES 6 TO 8.

At Serving Time:

Unmold on salad greens and serve with French dressing or mayonnaise.

Fish: Leaping Fresh
out of the Sea,
Can, or Freezer

In the past, one difficulty for most modern and hurried householders was the primary admonition, "first, catch your fish." Even when you weren't compelled to catch it yourself there was the ever-present problem of getting the fish when you wanted it and the even greater problem of cleaning, boning, skinning, and otherwise preparing it for the pan.

Enter the quick-frozen fillet, and the sad tale is ended. Quick-frozen fish has the advantage of being at least as fresh as the freshest, since the best brands are generally frozen within an hour or so after being caught. Equally important, such fish comes to the frozen-food lockers all ready to cook.

The quick-frozen fillet is presented here in a number of interesting classic guises. Each one of these dishes is achieved with a minimum of effort in the fewest possible minutes.

When using quick-frozen fish, you need not thaw beforehand. In several recipes we have suggested thawing only enough to separate the fillets. By this method the utmost in flavor is achieved, and furthermore there is no possibility of deterioration. If you thaw fish completely before cooking, remember that quick-frozen fish spoils as promptly as fresh. Never refreeze fish, and if you have leftover cooked fish, use it within 24 hours because it does not keep.

In addition to quick-frozen seafood there are, of course, the canned varieties, some of which are probably among the best known and most popular of canned foods. A large number of new products has been added to this category within the last few years—shad roe, for example, and prepared fish cakes. Salted, fresh, and dried fish in several forms are now presented so that they no longer require soaking or freshening.

So wide is the choice, so delicate are the flavors, that many individuals and families who once insisted, "We're not much for fish or seafood," have now completely changed their way of thinking. Whether you are a fish fancier or a nonfancier try some of our shortcuts. They may well become some of the most prized and often-repeated dishes in your repertoire.

Shibboleth Smasher

Refreeze?
Yes and No

Yes, you can refreeze frozen foods—sometimes.

As long as the contents of the package are still cold to the touch and food still contains ice crystals, at about 40° F., frozen foods can be refrozen with perfect safety. In a few cases there may be some loss of quality—some softening of texture and loss of flavor or color—compared to foods kept permanently frozen. There is, however, practically no danger in refreezing unopened packages of such foods.

Vegetables and meats take not too unkindly to refreezing. Fruits are less adaptable. In any case, you will probably want to use any refrozen foods as soon as possible.

Seafoods are tricky. Once defrosted, fish and seafood should be used as soon as possible.

Why do some packages bid you sternly "Do not refreeze"? Because the manufacturers want you to enjoy the foods at their best—they went to be sure their packages are used at the peak of goodness. Knowing the possibility of changes in texture and flavor occurring at defrost temperatures, they advise immediate use.

BROILED FISH

Thin pieces of fish do not need to be turned at all. Be careful when you are broiling fish not to overcook it. Don't try to get it very brown. The lightest tanning should suffice. Cook 4 inches from the source of heat if the broiler is on full force, or at moderate temperatures and only until the fish flakes off easily when touched with a fork and does not have any transparent look.

Small whole fish such as smelts or brook trout may be broiled. Bluefish, mackerel, pompano, or scrod are often merely split and broiled fresh-side-up without turning. Fillets of fish, salmon steaks, or halibut steaks may also be broiled and are turned only if they are quite thick.

Rinse fish in cold running water. Pat dry with paper towels. Brush with olive oil or salad oil.

Preheat broiler. Place fish on a well-greased rack. Sprinkle with salt and pepper. Dot with bits of butter or brush with olive or salad oil.

If you have trouble moving the fish without breaking it, try using 2 pancake turners or 2 broad spatulas.

FISH TEMPURA

Fish should be cleaned and scraped. Slice into pieces 2 to 3 inches in size and 3/8-inch thick. Smelts are often split, the heads and bones removed, leaving tails. Fifteen minutes before frying, sprinkle fish lightly with salt.

YOU WILL NEED:

Fish, smelts, or shrimp, 1/2 pound per
 person
Tempura batter (see below)
Oil, peanut or other

Heat oil (about 2 inches deep in electric fryer) to 300°–350° F. A tempura chef makes the testing of the temperature quite a ceremony, tossing a bit of batter from the end of his long cooking chopsticks into the oil with a dramatic gesture, listening to the spatter, and noting the time it takes to brown.

Prepare batter by beating 1 egg lightly and adding 2/3 cup water, then 1 cup flour and 1/2 teaspoon salt—beating gently but constantly with a fork or whip, or placing in blender 5 seconds. The batter should be quite thin.

Dip fish into batter and drop gently into oil. Fry until delicately golden.

SERVES 4.

At Serving Time:

Drain on paper towel and serve immediately.

FRAGRANT FISH CURRY

YOU WILL NEED:

4 packages frozen haddock in white
    wine sauce
2 tablespoons peanut oil
2 tablespoons finely chopped onion
1 clove garlic, finely sliced or crushed
    (optional)
2 teaspoons curry powder
1/3 cup tomato paste or catsup
Dash lemon juice
Chopped chives or parsley

Heat according to package directions 4 packages frozen haddock in white wine sauce. Meanwhile, heat in a dish that can go to the table 2 tablespoons peanut oil. Add 2 tablespoons finely chopped onion and 1 clove finely sliced or crushed garlic, if desired. When onions are golden but not at all brown, add 2 teaspoons curry powder and 1/3 cup tomato paste or tomato catsup, 1 tablespoon hot water, and a dash lemon juice. Stir and cook for another 3 or 4 minutes. Mix the heated haddock into the curry sauce, incorporating gently. Be careful not to deal roughly with the fish. It should be in eating pieces rather than in fillets.

SERVES 4.

At Serving Time:

Sprinkle curry with chopped chives or parsley, and serve with cooked rice and banana chutney.

SAUTÉED SCALLOPS

Each year in New Bedford, Massachusetts, home of the whalers, there is in late summer a scallop festival. Under green-striped tents are consumed tons of the seafood that the French call the coquilles, *or shells, of St. Jacques. Many people still harbor the illusion that scallops are punched-out pieces of fish. Never so! There are two kinds of scallops, the tiny bay variety (comparatively scarce and seasonal) and the larger sea scallops that can be obtained either fresh or frozen almost everywhere anytime. The trick about cooking scallops—like most seafood—can be expressed in two words: Don't overcook.*

YOU WILL NEED:

2 pounds fresh or frozen scallops
Flour
6 tablespoons olive oil
2 or 3 cloves garlic, crushed
1/2 teaspoon salt
1/8 teaspoon freshly ground black
   pepper
1/2 cup chopped parsley

If frozen scallops are used, they need not be completely thawed. To look like bay scallops, sea scallops should be cut into half-inch pieces. Wash and dry the scallops on paper towels. Roll in flour just enough to make a very thin coating.

Meanwhile place in blender 6 tablespoons olive oil and 2 or 3 cloves crushed garlic. Blend.

In the frying pan heat olive oil to 390° F. (use cooking thermometer if not using electric skillet), very hot. When light goes off, add scallops and cook very quickly, about 2 minutes, tossing them lightly in the hot oil. Sprinkle with 1/2 teaspoon salt and 1/8 teaspoon freshly ground pepper.

At Serving Time:

(Which should be immediately.) Add ½ cup chopped parsley. Toss parsley around so that scallops are nicely coated with it. Serve with lemon wedges and heated potato chips or julienne potato sticks. Parsley is most easily chopped by snipping it with scissors, or it can be done in the blender.

SHALLOW-DEEP FRIED FISH FILLETS

YOU WILL NEED:

4 frozen fillets of sole, halibut, ocean
   perch, flounder, or haddock
¾ cup flour
1 teaspoon salt
½ teaspoon freshly ground black
   pepper
Salad oil, peanut oil, or vegetable
   shortening
Parsley or watercress

Thaw 4 frozen fillets of sole, halibut, ocean perch, flounder, or haddock. Dip pieces of fish into ¾ cup flour seasoned with 1 teaspoon salt and ½ teaspoon freshly ground black pepper. In an electric skillet or deep, heavy frying pan, heat enough salad oil, peanut oil, or vegetable shortening to stand about 1½ inches deep. Allow oil to heat to 370° F. and let it stay at that temperature for 5 minutes. Then ease the fish into the oil. It will probably brown on both sides without having to be turned, but turn it if you like. Cook 5 minutes or until delicately golden. If you are not quite sure of doneness, test 1 piece with a fork. If done, the fish will flake easily. Remove with a slotted spoon. Drain on paper towels.

SERVES 4.

At Serving Time:

Serve on hot platter. Garnish with parsley or watercress.

POACHED SALMON—HOT OR COLD

This is one of the lordliest of gastronomic creations, but when you followed the classic methods it was difficult to achieve without a special yard-long fish kettle equipped with a rack. Our grandmothers, with large houses and acres of shelf space, could keep such a receptacle on hand for the salmon season. In addition to the kettle and rack, considerable knowledge and care were required to make sure that the court bouillon did not boil hard; otherwise the salmon would fall apart in strings. But we use our oven and a covered roaster or deep pan.

YOU WILL NEED:

1 whole salmon
Cheesecloth (optional)
Court bouillon (see Salmon Poached in
   White Wine, page 65, for directions)

Choose a fish that will fit on the rack in your roaster or deepish pan with head and tail intact—the ideal way. However, if you prefer, you may remove the head and tail. Wrap the fish, if you like, in a layer of cheesecloth. Add sufficient court bouillon to cover the fish, cover pan and set in a 350° oven. Simmer, covered, for about 10 minutes per pound or until fish is opaque and flakes easily when touched with a fork.

SERVES: COUNT ON A POUND OF FISH PER PERSON.

At Serving Time:

If you wish to serve the fish hot, simply lift it with the rack, remove cheesecloth, and serve with any favorite sauce. Hollandaise is one of the most revered accompaniments to salmon, as
. are boiled new potatoes and baby peas.

Variation:
Cold Poached Salmon

Allow salmon to cool in the court bouillon, then remove and serve with mayonnaise.

SALMON POACHED IN WHITE WINE

This is epicurean treatment for fresh or quick-frozen salmon steaks, halibut steaks, or fillets of flounder. Even canned salmon heated in this court bouillon is elegant.

YOU WILL NEED:

6 salmon, halibut, or flounder fillets
1 medium carrot
1 onion
2 stalks celery
2 tablespoons butter or margarine
2 sprigs parsley
4 or 5 peppercorns
2 cloves
1/2 bay leaf
1 tablespoon salt
2 tablespoons vinegar
1 tablespoon lemon juice
2 quarts white wine or part white wine
  and part water

Chop 1 medium-sized carrot, 1 onion, and 2 stalks of celery, and cook all together in 2 tablespoons butter or margarine along with 2 sprigs parsley for about 3 minutes. Add 4 or 5 peppercorns, 2 cloves, 1/2 bay leaf, 1 tablespoon salt, 2 tablespoons vinegar, 1 tablespoon lemon juice, and 2 quarts white wine or use half water, half wine or any desired proportion of wine to water—depending on your taste. Boil uncovered about 10 minutes.

Lay the fish gently into the court bouillon. Turn down the heat and simmer 6 to 10 minutes per pound. The exact time depends upon the thickness of the fish. When done, the fish will have lost its transparent look and will flake off easily at the touch of a fork. Allow to cool in its own broth. You may keep and use this bouillon for a few days for poaching other fish.

SERVES 6. COUNT ON ABOUT 1/2 POUND PER PORTION.

At Serving Time:

Provide mayonnaise or hollandaise sauce and boiled potatoes.

SALMON MOUSSE

For the most tremendous drama, you could make this mousse at the table and serve it immediately, mounded on crisp lettuce for individual portions, or even more dramatically, inside a large spread-out heart of Boston or romaine lettuce.

YOU WILL NEED:

1/2 cup hot water
2 envelopes unflavored gelatin
1/4 cup cut-up onion
1 (8-ounce) can salmon
2 egg yolks or 1 whole egg
1 tablespoon lemon juice
1/8 teaspoon pepper
Cayenne pepper or Tabasco
1 cup finely crushed ice
1 cup heavy cream
Peanut oil
Red food coloring (optional)

Put 1/2 cup hot water into blender with 2 envelopes unflavored gelatin. Cover and blend 40 seconds. Add 1/4 cup cut-up onion, 1 (8-ounce) can salmon, and 2 egg yolks or 1 whole egg. Cover and blend 5 seconds. Add 1 tablespoon lemon juice, 1/8 teaspoon pepper, a few grains cayenne pepper or 2 drops Tabasco. Blend 5 seconds longer. With motor on, remove cover; add 1 cup finely crushed ice, 1 cup heavy cream, and if desired, a couple of drops of red food coloring. Continue to blend for 40 seconds or until mousse begins to thicken. Serve immediately as suggested above. Or have ready a quart-size mold, which should be cold and rinsed with water or lightly brushed with peanut oil. Quick-chill in the freezing compartment 5 minutes, until mixture is set, or in the refrigerator about an hour.

At Serving Time:

Have plenty of crisp greens, quartered tomatoes, sliced cucumbers, and if you're feeling extremely elegant, some slices of truffles.

STEAMED FISH, CHINESE-STYLE

An old-fashioned roaster or a deep, wide pan with cover takes the place of special steaming equipment.

YOU WILL NEED:

2 tablespoons peanut or salad oil
1 tablespoon sherry or Madeira
1 tablespoon soy sauce
1/2 small white onion
6 dried mushrooms
White fish, 1/2 pound per person
White pepper
Chopped chives or scallion tops

Place in blender 2 tablespoons peanut or salad oil, 1 tablespoon dry sherry or Madeira, 1 tablespoon soy sauce, 1/2 small white onion cut into pieces, 6 small dried mushrooms that have been soaked in warm water for at least 1/2 hour. Blend 2 or 3 seconds.

Rub fish on all sides with white pepper and sprinkle sauce on all sides of fish. Then sprinkle with chopped chives or scallion tops. Pour into roaster pan 2 inches of boiling water. When water is steaming in a lively fashion, place fish on an ovenproof platter and lower onto rack set above boiling water. Cook, covered, 10 to 15 minutes for a fish 2 inches thick; cook 4 to 6 minutes for fish fillets or small fish steaks.

At Serving Time:

Serve with rice.

STEAMED LOBSTER

A covered roaster is ideal for an old-fashioned New England lobster bake. Six, eight, or even ten small lobsters may be steamed at once. If you can get some rock weed, place it on top of the lobsters. It does give a delightful flavor. Rock weed, by the way, can be kept in plastic bags in your freezer and reused two or three times.

YOU WILL NEED:

Whole fresh live lobsters (1 to 1½
   pounds is considered ideal size for
   flavor and tenderness)
Rock weed (optional)
New England Butter Sauce (see page
   69)

For each person allow 1 lobster weighing from 1 to 1½ pounds. They should be moving about in a lively fashion. If you must keep the lobsters around the house for a few hours, place them in a bag with ice in the refrigerator.

Cover bottom of roaster with boiling water 1 inch deep. Place live lobsters on rack. Cover and steam from 15 to 18 minutes or until lobster turns pink. Count cooking time after steaming starts.

At Serving Time:

Remove lobster from kettle onto a wooden board and place on its back. Split lengthwise with a heavy, sharp knife or Chinese cleaver, running it from the mouth through the body and tail. Remove the dark vein and intestinal sack. Frequently the underdeveloped spawn, or coral, which is a deep coral pink in color, will be found in the lobster and this is, in most people's opinion, the very best tidbit of all. Do not remove it. Crack the large claws. Serve lobster in the shells with New England Butter Sauce.

NEW ENGLAND BUTTER SAUCE

The required adjunct to steamed lobster or clams.

YOU WILL NEED:

1/2 pound butter
2 teaspoons lemon juice
1/2 teaspoon freshly ground black
   pepper
Tabasco or cayenne
1/2 teaspoon curry powder or celery
   seed

Melt 1/2 pound stick butter in electric saucepan, setting temperature at 200° F. (simmer). Do not allow it to boil. Add 2 teaspoons lemon juice, 1/2 teaspoon freshly ground black pepper, 2 or 3 drops Tabasco or a few grains of cayenne pepper, and 1/2 teaspoon curry powder or celery seed. Allow to stand in electric saucepan at about 150° for at least 1/2 hour to blend and mellow.

SERVES 4.

At Serving Time:

Pour into individual cups or ramekins.

QUICK LOBSTER NEWBURG

Lobster à la Newburg has a French sound, but actually it belongs to the New York of Delmonico's and the old Waldorf Peacock Alley. As the story goes, this dish was composed by one of Delmonico's chefs for an expansive gentleman whose name was Wenberg. Came a parting of the ways between Mr. Wenberg and his erstwhile favorite haunt—the restaurant, still wishing to feature the glorious concoction on their menu, changed the Wen to New and so it has been Lobster Newburg to this day. Our recipe is not the classic version, and it may not be authentic Wen- or Newburg, but it is powerfully good. Furthermore, this is not nearly so rich or calorific as the straight cream-and-butter version.

YOU WILL NEED:

2 cups cooked, canned, or quick-
   frozen lobster meat
1 can condensed cream of mushroom
   soup
1/4 to 1/2 soup-can dry sherry or sherry
   mixed with milk or light cream
1 egg, slightly beaten
Paprika (optional)

Start with 2 cups cooked lobster meat, canned or quick-frozen. The pieces should be good-sized, about 3/4 inch at least. Combine with 1 can condensed cream of mushroom soup, 1/4 to 1/2 soup-can dry sherry, or you may use equal parts milk or cream and sherry. Heat but do not boil. Beat 1 egg slightly with a fork. Dip a little of the hot sauce into the egg and stir. This is to prevent the egg from curdling. Add the egg-and-sauce mixture to the lobster. A touch of paprika may be added, just enough to make the sauce pink.

SERVES 6.

At Serving Time:

Serve at once, if possible from a chafing dish, and add to each portion a few grains nutmeg. Serve with rice or on toast, or garnished with heated, canned julienne potato sticks.

SHRIMP JAMBALAYA

Truly one of the great Creole dishes of Louisiana, this probably was originally known as French Jambon à la Riz. Many ingredients such as New Orleans breakfast sausage, oysters, and a large variety of spices can go into a jambalaya. Our simplified version uses ham, shrimp, and rice.

YOU WILL NEED:

2 medium-sized onions, chopped
2 tablespoons butter or bacon fat
1 cup ham, cut into 1/2-inch squares or
    julienne strips
2 cups canned or quick-frozen shrimp
1 clove garlic, crushed
Red pepper or Tabasco sauce
1 tablespoon chopped fresh parsley or
    1 teaspoon parsley flakes
1/2 teaspoon thyme
1 1/3 cups quick-cooking rice
2 cups tomato juice or canned
    vegetable juice
Salt to taste

Brown 2 medium-sized onions, chopped, in 2 tablespoons butter
or bacon fat. Add 1 cup ham cut into 1/2-inch squares or into thin
julienne strips and 2 cups cooked canned or quick-frozen
shrimp. Allow this mixture to simmer in a covered pan about 5
minutes, then add 1 clove crushed garlic, a few grains of red
pepper or 3 or 4 dashes of Tabasco sauce, 1 tablespoon freshly
chopped parsley or 1 teaspoon parsley flakes, 1/2 teaspoon
thyme, 1 package (1 1/3 cups) quick-cooking rice, and 2 cups
tomato or vegetable juice , salt to taste. Bring to a full boil
uncovered; allow to cook 2 or 3 minutes. Cover and let stand 10
minutes longer. (Cooked ham may be used, but the flavor is not
so rich.)

SERVES 6.

At Serving Time:

Fluff with a fork. Serve with a tossed green salad and dessert.
This makes a full and satisfying meal.

SCAMPI ALLA ROMANA

YOU WILL NEED:

2 buds garlic, chopped
1/4 pound shallots, chopped (white
    onions can be used in a pinch)
1/2 pound butter or margarine
1 tablespoon Worcestershire sauce
1/2 teaspoon Tabasco sauce
1 tablespoon chopped parsley
24 frozen jumbo shrimp or 36
    medium-size shrimp

Chop 2 buds garlic and 1/4 pound shallots or white onions very, very fine, and mix with 1/2 pound softened butter or margarine. Add 1 tablespoon Worcestershire sauce, 1/2 teaspoon Tabasco sauce, and 1 tablespoon chopped parsley. Mix thoroughly. Place 24 frozen jumbo shrimp or 36 medium-sized shrimp, leaving tail on, on heatproof platter and spread over them some of the butter mixture. Cook under broiler for about 10 minutes, turning occasionally. When nearly done, add more butter mixture and return to broil for 5 minutes more. When done, add rest of butter mixture and leave for a few minutes under the broiler, which has been turned off.

SERVES 6.

At Serving Time:

Remove from broiler, serve a glass of dry white wine, and serve immediately with crusty bread.

QUICK BALTIMORE DEVILED CRAB

If this be treason—to concoct Baltimore's own deviled crab from quick-

frozen crabmeat and cream of mushroom soup—make the best of it, and very good it is!

YOU WILL NEED:

2 to 2½ cups canned or quick-frozen
  crabmeat
1 cup undiluted condensed cream of
  mushroom soup
1 tablespoon chili sauce
2 teaspoons Worcestershire sauce
1 teaspoon chopped fresh parsley
Dash pepper
1 egg
½ teaspoon dry mustard
1 teaspoon lemon juice
¼ teaspoon salt
½ cup fine bread crumbs
Butter or salad oil
Parsley sprigs

To fill 6 medium-sized shells you will need 2 to 2½ cups crabmeat. Combine this amount of crabmeat with 1 cup undiluted condensed cream of mushroom soup heated in the top of a double boiler. Season with 1 tablespoon chili sauce, 2 teaspoons Worcestershire sauce, 1 teaspoon chopped parsley, and a dash pepper. Place the mixture in 6 crab shells or individual baking dishes; cover with a paste made of 1 egg beaten with ½ teaspoon dry mustard, 1 teaspoon lemon juice, ¼ teaspoon salt, and ½ cup fine bread crumbs. Brush liberally with melted butter or salad oil and bake at 350° F. until a rich brown, about 25 minutes.

SERVES 6.

At Serving Time:

Garnish with a sprig of parsley in the middle of each crab. Serve warm or cold.

LEMON-GLAZED HALIBUT

YOU WILL NEED:

2 pounds frozen halibut steaks
1/2 teaspoon salt
1 package lemon-flavored gelatin
    dissolved in 1 cup boiling water
Pinch ground saffron
1 cup commercial sour cream
Few sprigs fresh dill

Let 2 pounds frozen halibut steaks stand at room temperature 30 minutes. Fill a large skillet with 1 1/2 inches boiling water and add 1/2 teaspoon salt. Lower halibut into boiling water, reduce heat, and simmer 10 minutes or until halibut is white and flaky. Remove with slotted spatula and lift out center bone. Set aside to cook. Meanwhile, dissolve 1 package lemon-flavored gelatin in 1 cup boiling water and refrigerate until syrupy. Then add pinch ground saffron to 1 cup commercial sour cream and fold into gelatin. Spoon over cooled halibut, spreading evenly with spatula. Garnish with a few sprigs fresh dill and refrigerate until coating is firm.

SERVES 6.

At Serving Time:

Serve on platter with fluted lemon cups filled with Russian salad or cucumber cups with coleslaw.

OVEN-FRIED FILLETS

When you don't want to go to the trouble of deep-fat frying, or when you want to fix quite a few servings all at once, try the quick trick of oven-frying. This method is adaptable to all types of fillets and for small fish, such as smelts or porgies, that are fried whole.

YOU WILL NEED:

1 (1-pound) package quick-frozen fish
  fillets
1/4 cup milk
Soft bread crumbs seasoned with salt,
  pepper, and paprika
2 tablespoons melted butter or salad or
  olive oil
Parsley or watercress sprigs
Lemon or lime wedges

Thaw a 1-pound box of quick-frozen fish fillets just enough to separate. Dip in milk, using about 1/4 cup; roll in bread crumbs seasoned with salt and pepper. A little paprika added to the bread crumbs provides an extra-pretty brown. Place the fish in a buttered or oiled baking dish, preferably one that can go to the table. Sprinkle with 2 tablespoons melted butter or salad or olive oil. Bake in a hot oven, 450°, about 20 minutes, or until done.

SERVES 2.

At Serving Time:

Garnish with parsley or watercress and wedges of lemon or lime.

The Bird

Some of the best and also some of the worst ready-to-serve canned and quick-frozen foods are chicken products. Perhaps one reason for the wide disparity in quality may be the enormous variety of brands, manufacturers, and cooking techniques. Find a good brand and never give it up—or at least not unless it becomes evident that there has been a change in management and a consequent change in quality. (Sad to say, this sometimes happens.)

In addition to the ubiquitous canned and quick-frozen chicken à la king, which is useful in so many guises, you should acquaint yourself with canned chicken fricassee, in which, as in the old-time Sunday dinner, the chicken is left on the bones.

Still another boon to the time-pressed cook is quick-frozen poultry that is cleaned, cut up, and all ready to be thawed and cooked. And blessings on the practical genius who first thought of selling chicken parts!

You no longer need to own a poultry farm or shares in a fancy restaurant to be able to enjoy breasts of chicken supreme—whenever you have a mind for it.

Prepared poultry dishes in one form or another can often be used as the beginning of more unusual and distinguished dishes.

It is important to remember, however, that cooked poultry dishes of any description (home-cooked, frozen, deli, rotisseried, or a "basket full of fried") may become more than unpalatable—in fact downright dangerous—if allowed to stand too long at room temperature. "Buy" them hot-off-the-fire or straight from the refrigerator.

With this warning in mind, have fun!

CHICKEN CACCIATORE WITH WHITE WINE AND OLIVES

There are hundreds of versions. This one is subtle and elegant.

YOU WILL NEED:

2 packages frozen chicken cacciatore
¼ cup white wine
¼ cup ripe black olives
¼ cup green olives
1 clove garlic
Rice or polenta
Grated Parmesan cheese
Parsley sprigs
Anchovy fillets (optional)

Heat 2 packages frozen chicken cacciatore according to package directions. Meanwhile, in a small bowl combine ¼ cup white wine; ¼ cup ripe black olives, pitted and diced or sliced; and ¼ cup green olives, which may or may not be stuffed with pimientos. Season with 1 clove garlic put through the press. Add to chicken cacciatore and bring just to a boil.

SERVES 2.

At Serving Time:

Serve with rice or polenta (basically, cornmeal mush) into which a little grated Parmesan cheese may be stirred. Garnish with parsley, and if desired, some fillets of anchovy.

CHICKEN LIVERS SATÉ

This recipe was originally intended for charcoal hibachis, but I have discovered that it can be done just as well on a regular broiler. This makes a delightful hors d'oeuvre.

YOU WILL NEED:

1 cup dry sherry or vermouth
$^1/_2$ cup soy sauce
2 tablespoons sugar
1 pound chicken livers, cut into $^3/_4$-
   inch pieces
Peanut oil
Ground ginger (optional)
Melba toast rounds

Bring close to a boil but do not boil (merely keep at a slow, gentle simmer) 1 cup dry sherry or vermouth, $^1/_2$ cup soy sauce, and 2 tablespoons sugar—or use a sweeter sherry or vermouth and omit sugar. Cool 5 minutes. Pour over 1 pound chicken livers cut into $^3/_4$-inch pieces. Allow to stand covered for about 1 hour at room temperature or several hours in refrigerator. Place on skewers or well separated on a piece of greased aluminum foil. Brush livers with peanut oil. Broil 5 minutes or less if need be. Livers must not be overcooked.

SERVES 4.

At Serving Time:

If desired, sprinkle lightly with ground ginger. Spear with toothpicks or serve on Melba toast rounds.

Variation:

Chicken livers for luncheon, may be prepared in exactly the same way and served with rice and a green vegetable.

CHICKEN OR TURKEY PIES

YOU WILL NEED:

Frozen turkey pies (1 per serving)

Sweet cream or commercial sour
  cream
Chopped chives or parsley

Heat frozen turkey pies according to package directions. Five minutes before removing from the oven, brush tops with sweet cream or commercial sour cream.

At Serving Time:

Sprinkle with chopped chives or parsley.

CHICKEN PAPRIKA

This is an unorthodox but delightfully flavored version of a famous Hungarian specialty.

YOU WILL NEED:

Butter or margarine
1 onion, sliced
1 tablespoon Hungarian paprika
1 can chicken fricassee
1/4 cup sour cream

Thinly slice and gently fry in butter or margarine 1 medium onion. Add 1 tablespoon Hungarian paprika and 1/4 cup water. Allow the onion to become thoroughly soft and golden, then add 1 can chicken fricassee. Heat thoroughly and stir in 1/4 cup sour cream. Do not boil after the cream is in.

SERVES 2.

At Serving Time:

Serve immediately with buttered wide noodles scattered with poppy seeds or slivered almonds, which are available in cans.

BROILED CHICKEN WITH WHITE WINE AND TARRAGON

White wine, herbs, plenty of butter, and slow cooking are the secrets of this exquisite food.

YOU WILL NEED:

2 (2-pound) broilers or fryers,
   quartered
Salt and pepper
1/4 cup butter or salad oil
1/2 cup dry white wine
1/2 teaspoon dried tarragon or
   rosemary
2 tablespoons each chopped chives and
   parsley
Parsley or watercress sprigs

Sprinkle quartered broilers or fryers with salt and pepper and rub well on all sides with butter or salad oil. Arrange on well-greased broiler grid, flesh side up toward the heat. Place at least 1 tablespoonful of butter on each piece. Broil 5 or 6 inches from the heat. This will take about 20 to 25 minutes on each side. Finish the broiling with the skin side up.

Meanwhile, prepare a basting sauce, using 1/4 cup butter, 1/2 cup dry white wine, 1/2 teaspoon dried tarragon or rosemary, and 2 tablespoons each chopped chives and parsley. Baste the chicken as it broils with this sauce.

SERVES 4.

At Serving Time:

Garnish with bouquets of parsley or watercress.

Variation:

Rock Cornish game hens split for broiling can be prepared in the same way.

DEVILED CHICKEN

Easily made, this joy of the Southland is a perfect choice for a meal that may have to wait. It can be kept warm for a long time in a very slow oven or reheated when needed.

YOU WILL NEED:

1 (1½-pound) quick-frozen frying
  chicken
Dry mustard
1 tablespoon Worcestershire sauce
1 cup wine vinegar
1 teaspoon sugar
Butter, margarine, or olive oil
Chopped parsley

Thaw chicken, preferably in hot oven, then place on a shallow ovenproof pan. Rub with dry mustard. Sprinkle with 1 table-spoon Worcestershire sauce. Pour over 1 cup wine vinegar diluted with ½ cup water and 1 teaspoon sugar. Bake 30 minutes in moderate oven, 350° F., basting once or twice. Just before serving dot with butter or margarine, or brush with olive oil and set under the broiler just long enough to turn a pretty golden brown.

SERVES 2.

At Serving Time:

Sprinkle with chopped parsley and serve the chicken with fluffy boiled rice.

REVOLUTIONARY BIRD-ROASTING

Before you start, calculate how long it will take the bird to cook. Figure on 20 minues per pound. If poultry is frozen it will take from 1½ to 2 times the usual length of time. (Allow ½ hour for bird to rest warmly before the feast—essential for swift, neat slicing.)

Let's assume your meat is solidly frozen. Give it a drugstore wrap in heavy-duty foil. Stow in a moderately hot 375° F. oven. A large roasting chicken should thaw in the oven in about 1 hour; a small turkey (8 to 10 pounds) in 1½ hours. When bird is thawed, it will be easy to pull out the giblets in their paper wrappings. Wipe inside and out with a warm damp cloth or towel and rub with softened butter or margarine blended with a touch of cognac, bourbon, or wine. Into the cave, poke a quartered, unpeeled onion with a clove stuck in each section, along with a handful of celery tops and 1 lemon, washed and cut in half. Pin the wings and legs to the sides with short skewers. Tuck the neck skin underneath against the rack (no pins are needed). Place a tent of heavy-duty foil over the bird. Now, back to the oven— until the little built-in gadget some lucky turkeys have, pops out, or the drumstick wiggles easily and the meat feels springy. You can, of course, rely on a meat thermometer if you have one. Be sure to push it into solid flesh—not touching bone. Most people overcook poultry. No matter who tells you differently, the thermometer should register no more than 185° F. In spite of thousands of printed recipes, most fine chefs agree on this point. Twenty minutes before "done time," remove tent for final crisp browning.

ROAST DUCK BIGARADE

Since quick-frozen Long Island ducklings have become so widely available, they are an excellent choice for company dinner.

YOU WILL NEED:

1 (3½- to 5-pound) quick-frozen Long
   Island duckling
2 medium onions, quartered
8 cloves
¼ cup orange juice
½ teaspoon Kitchen Bouquet
Cayenne

1 tablespoon orange marmalade
1 package prepared beef gravy
1 or 2 tablespoons brandy (optional)
Watercress
Orange slices

Thaw duckling. Instead of stuffing the duck, place inside it 2 onions peeled and quartered, each quarter studded with a single clove. Roast uncovered 1½ to 2 hours at 375° F. About 15 minutes before the duck is done, brush lightly with Kitchen Bouquet.

SERVES 3 TO 4.

BIGARADE SAUCE

Prepare Bigarade Sauce by heating together ¼ cup orange juice, ½ teaspoon Kitchen Bouquet, a few grains cayenne, 1 tablespoon orange marmalade, and 1 can prepared beef gravy. If desired, 1 or 2 tablespoons brandy may be added to the sauce. Simmer gently about 4 minutes.

At Serving Time:
Roast Duck Bigarade may be served in either of two ways— brought to the table whole and carved like any poultry or cut into serving pieces beforehand, arranged on the serving dish with the sauce poured around the duck. A bouquet of fresh watercress makes a pretty garnish. Thin slices of unpeeled orange are also used.

INDONESIAN DRUMSTICKS

An unusual but simple way to glamorize chicken legs. Wings or second joints may be used, and Chicken Livers Saté (see pages 77-78) may be served as appetizers.

YOU WILL NEED:

1/2 cup soy sauce
1/2 cup honey
1 clove garlic or small piece green
    ginger root, crushed
12 frozen chicken drumsticks
Almonds, peanuts, or hazelnuts
Sesame seeds

Combine 1/2 cup each soy sauce, honey, and hot water. Add 1 clove garlic or small piece green ginger root, crushed. Stir thoroughly and brush over a dozen frozen chicken drumsticks which have been thawed. Allow to stand at room temperature at least 1 hour. Place the drumsticks on greased aluminum foil. Broil 4 inches away from the heat until the meat looks opaque, about 20 minutes. Count on 1 to 2 drumsticks to serve each person as an entrée.

SERVES 6.

At Serving Time:

Have on hand 1 small bowl chopped nuts—almonds, peanuts, or hazelnuts—and another little bowl of sesame seeds. The chicken is dipped first in the nuts and then into the sesame seeds. Thin slices of homemade or old-fashioned white bread make an ideal accompaniment.

DUCK IN ASPIC AU COINTREAU

For a summer buffet, this dish is outstanding and very easy to prepare.

YOU WILL NEED:

1 (3 1/2-pound) quick-frozen Long
    Island duckling
1 orange
1 onion
4 cloves

2 tablespoons honey
1/2 teaspoon Kitchen Bouquet
2 (10³/4-ounce) cans consommé
3 tablespoons Cointreau or sherry
Peaches, apples, or pears, sliced
Cinnamon

Thaw duckling. Stuff with 1 quartered orange and 1 quartered onion. Spear each onion quarter with a clove. Roast uncovered in a shallow pan 1½ to 2 hours at 375° F. About 15 minutes before duck is done, brush with 2 tablespoons honey combined with ½ teaspoon Kitchen Bouquet to give the bird a beautiful golden-brown gloss. Cool to room temperature. Cut with poultry shears into serving pieces.

Arrange duckling in a shallow 10 x 6-inch serving dish. Pour over 2 cans undiluted condensed consommé to which you have added 3 tablespoons Cointreau. If you do not have Cointreau, use a pale sherry. Allow to stand in the refrigerator until consommé has jelled.

SERVES 2.

At Serving Time:

Bring to the table in the same dish in which it has jelled. Decorate with sliced peaches, apples, or pears. Sprinkle delicately with cinnamon. A bouquet of crisp escarole or watercress looks pretty at one side or in the center.

Meaty Matter

Because meat is frequently the most time-consuming as well as the costliest part of the menu, the time- and money-saving recipes and suggestions in this chapter will, we hope, be of help to you. Within this field great strides have been made. Your local chain store or favorite delicatessen has a wide variety of meat specialties—lamb and veal as well as beef in stews, beef and kidneys ready for an English steak and kidney pie, several types of meatballs presented in a variety of sauces, all sorts of meat pies, pot roasts, meats in gravy. If you are careful to select some of the best-known brands you should be agreeably surprised at the good flavor of many canned meats.

In a number of cases manufacturers have been singularly successful in avoiding or disguising a canned flavor. But even the best, in our opinion, may be greatly improved—the taste freshened and flavor heightened—by herbs, spices, and/or wine or sour cream.

Many canned meats and gravies are not particularly attractive to look at. They may have a grayish or drab brick color, but this can easily be changed into the deep, glossy brown of a French ragout by the addition of widely available bottled gravy darkeners, such as Kitchen Bouquet or Gravymaster. These products contain some spices but the base is caramelized sugar, which does not sweeten food. However, if you use too much you might get a slightly bitter taste. So add it little by little.

Most helpful to the hurried cook with a small family are ready-cooked meats—sliced roasts and baked hams—that are generally available at delicatessens, whose owners always seem to prefer to sell them in sandwiches but can sometimes be persuaded to omit the bread. Buy thick slices and you can embark on a series of dishes that were formerly available only to those who first "roasted a joint."

May we reiterate that many recipes included in this group are economical and need no last-minute fussing.

BEEF STEW WITH WINE

Several good beginnings for beef stew are available in cans. Few are savory enough to serve as is. But the additions suggested here will improve them.

YOU WILL NEED:

1 can beef stew
$1/2$ teaspoon Kitchen Bouquet
1 to 2 tablespoons red wine
$1/2$ to 1 clove garlic
$1/2$ teaspoon marjoram or oregano
Parsley (optional)

To a can of beef stew, add $1/2$ teaspoon Kitchen Bouquet; 1 to 2 tablespoons red wine, or a little more if you wish; $1/2$ to 1 clove garlic, well crushed; and/or $1/2$ teaspoon dried marjoram or oregano. Simmer (do not boil) at least 5 minutes to blend the flavors.

SERVES 2.

At Serving Time:

Serve in heated casserole. Stew should be bubbling hot. A tablespoon of finely chopped parsley may be sprinkled on the top to give that homemade appearance and a fresh flavor.

BEEF TONGUE VISTULA

Cooked beef tongue from the deli or bought in a jar is much better without any extra cooking. Simply cover with boiling sauce and allow to stand in a warm place about five minutes.

YOU WILL NEED:

12 slices cooked beef tongue
1 (10½-ounce) can beef gravy
¼ cup red wine vinegar
1 teaspoon grated lemon rind
½ cup raisins
½ cup chopped nuts

Lay 12 slices cooked beef tongue into bubbling hot sauce made by heating together 1 can beef gravy, ¼ cup red wine vinegar, ½ cup raisins, ½ cup chopped nuts, and 1 teaspoon grated lemon rind. Allow to warm thoroughly.

SERVES 4.

At Serving Time:

Present around a mound or in a ring of whipped potatoes, rice, or polenta (cornmeal mush).

BAKED CORNED BEEF HASH DE LUXE

Many and varied are the varieties of corned beef hash on the market. Shop around for a brand with a low proportion of potato. Dress it up like this.

YOU WILL NEED:

1 (16 ounce) can corned beef hash
2 tablespoons raw onion
2 tablespoons milk, ketchup, or chili
    sauce
½ cup diced beets (optional)
Butter
Parsley

To a (16-ounce) can corned beef hash, add 2 tablespoons finely chopped raw onion, 2 tablespoons milk, ketchup, or chili sauce. Add ½ cup finely diced cooked beets if desired. Butter generously a shallow casserole or pie pan. Spread hash in the pan. Dot with butter. Bake in a moderate oven, 350°F., until piping hot and crusty underneath, about 20 to 25 minutes.

SERVES 4.

At Serving Time:

Sprinkle with chopped parsley and serve piping hot from the baking dish.

DRIED BEEF AND CELERY SAUCE

This is a fine main dish for a late breakfast or a light supper.

YOU WILL NEED:

¼ pound dried beef
1 can condensed cream of celery soup
½ soup can milk or light cream
½ teaspoon dehydrated horseradish
1 tablespoon brandy (optional)
Toast or English muffins
Parsley, chives, or almonds

Cover ¼ pound dried beef with a little cold water and bring to a boil. Take from the stove and let stand for about 5 minutes. This removes the excess salt from the beef and softens it. Drain and add to a can of condensed cream of celery soup that has been diluted with ½ can water, milk, or light cream. Stir in ½ teaspoon dehydrated horseradish. The addition of 1 tablespoon brandy to the sauce will add piquancy, for a particularly elegant effect with no suggestion of a liquor flavor. Heat slowly, stirring once or twice.

SERVES 4.

At Serving Time:

Serve on toast or English muffins. Sprinkle with chopped parsley, chives or whole toasted almonds.

BEEF STROGANOFF

YOU WILL NEED:

1 (2-pound) filet of beef
2 tablespoons butter or margarine
1/2 tablespoon minced onion
1/2 pound mushrooms
Salt
Nutmeg
1/2 pint sour cream

Filet should be cut in 1/2-inch slices. Pound filet with wooden mallet or potato masher to make very thin and cut in neat finger-shaped pieces. Melt 2 tablespoons butter or margarine, add 1/2 tablespoon minced onion and cook and stir until onion is yellow. Add beef. Cook quickly about 3 minutes, turning the pieces to brown on all sides; set aside. Slice down vertically 1/2 pound mushrooms and sauté in remaining butter. Season with salt and a few grains nutmeg and add to beef.

SERVES 6.

At Serving Time:

Add 1/2 pint sour cream, heat and season delicately to taste. Steamed wild rice is excellent as a border for this dish.

BEEF BOURGUIGNON

YOU WILL NEED:

4 packages frozen beef with onions in
   red wine
12 small white onions or 1 (8-ounce)
   can white onions, drained
Butter or margarine
1 (6-ounce) can whole or sliced
   mushrooms
1 tablespoon cognac
1 clove garlic (optional)
1/8 teaspoon each cinnamon, clove,
   nutmeg, and ginger
Chopped parsley
White bread

Heat 4 packages frozen beef with onions in red wine, according
to package directions. Meanwhile, brown a dozen small white
onions or 1 well-drained 8-ounce can white onions in butter or
margarine. Add a 6-ounce can of whole, sliced, or diced
mushrooms with liquid. Add 1 cup hot water, 1 tablespoon
cognac, 1 clove garlic if desired, and 1/8 teaspoon each cinnamon,
clove, nutmeg, and ginger. Combine with the heated stew and
allow to simmer together for a few minutes.

SERVES 4.

At Serving Time:

Sprinkle generously with chopped parsley. Garnish with trian-
gles of bread that have been browned in butter or toasted and
buttered on both sides.

BIGOS

Blessed fate for canned, leftover, or deli ham is Poland's heroic Hunter's Stew—the lordly Bigos.

YOU WILL NEED:

2 cups cooked ham
1 cup Kielbasi sausage
1 package onion-soup mix
1 can condensed tomato soup
1 cup red wine
2 (16-ounce) cans sauerkraut
2 slices bacon
8 dried mushrooms
1 cup apple-pie slices
1 bay leaf
1/2 teaspoon cracked black
   peppercorns

Bring to boil 2 cups diced cooked ham; 1 cup Kielbasi sausage; 1 can condensed tomato soup; 1 package onion-soup mix; 5 cups water; 1 cup red wine; 2 pounds well-rinsed sauerkraut; 2 slices bacon, snipped; 8 dried mushrooms, soaked till soft; 1 cup canned apple-pie slices, drained; and 1 bay leaf, crumbled; 1/2 teaspoon cracked black peppercorns. Cook briskly 15 minutes. Cover and simmer till you are ready to eat.

SERVES 6 TO 8.

At Serving Time:

Ladle from tureen or casserole into deep soup plates or bowls and serve with boiled potatoes and/or sour rye bread.

PIROSHKI

The French have their "tartelettes" of puff paste, the English their "pasties." The Spaniards and Brazilians call them "empanados." In the

West Indies, pepper-hot, they become "pates." In Slavic lands they take unto themselves a variety of different shapes, sizes, and fillings. The big ones are called "pirogen"; the small ones, "piroshki." All are admirable accompaniments to any soup. We use for the crusty part a package of ready-to-bake refrigerator biscuits; and for the filling, strained canned beef or some finely chopped leftover beef.

YOU WILL NEED:

10 refrigerator biscuits
3 (½-oz.) cans strained canned beef or
   ½ cup finely chopped cooked meat,
   chicken, or seafood
2 hard-cooked eggs
2 tablespoons butter or margarine
1 small onion
Salt and pepper

Ten biscuits already rolled and cut are in the package. Cut each in half crosswise. Flatten with the hand so that they are about 3 inches in diameter. On one side of each, place a teaspoonful of filling made by combining 3 (½-ounce) cans strained beef for infants, or use about ½ cup finely chopped cooked meat, chicken, or seafood, 2 coarsely chopped hard-cooked eggs, 2 tablespoons softened butter or margarine, and 1 small onion, very finely chopped. Add salt and pepper to taste. Mix well. Fold dough over to make half-moons and press down the edges with a fork. Brush with beaten egg. Bake about 10 minutes at 450° F.

MAKES 20.

At Serving Time:

Serve hot with soup or salad.

CALIFORNIA CHILI

A little extra garlic and paprika, a teaspoon of cumin seed, provide authentic flavor for canned chili.

YOU WILL NEED:

2 15-ounce cans chili con carne with
   beans, or 1 can chili and 1 can red
   kidney beans
2 cloves garlic
1 tablespoon paprika
1 teaspoon cumin seed
Chopped parsley or chives

Crush well 2 cloves garlic and combine with 2 cans chili con carne with beans or 1 can chili (meat) and 1 can cooked red kidney beans. Season with 1 tablespoon paprika and 1 teaspoon cumin seed. Heat, stirring occasionally.

SERVES 2 TO 4.

At Serving Time:

Serve with celery, dill pickles, and crackers. Or place the chili mixture inside a ring of cooked rice or cooked yellow cornmeal mush. Sprinkle with chopped parsley or chives.

INTOXICATED PORK CHOPS

Doused with a generous quaff of Marsala, these pork chops are a marvel for speed and elegance, especially if you use the thinly sliced brown-and-serve type.

YOU WILL NEED:

8 brown-and-serve pork chops
1 tablespoon butter
1 tablespoon olive oil
1 cup Marsala wine
1 clove garlic
1 tablespoon tomato paste
1/2 cup condensed canned consommé
Parsley

Season 8 thin brown-and-serve pork chops with salt and pepper. Brown in 1 tablespoon butter and 1 tablespoon olive oil about 5 minutes on each side. Add 1 cup Marsala wine; 1 clove garlic, crushed; 1 tablespoon tomato paste; 1/2 cup condensed canned consommé, undiluted. Cook about 5 minutes longer.

SERVES 4.

At Serving Time:

Sprinkle generously with chopped parsley and serve immediately.

Shibboleth Smasher

Frozen meats would be a hundred times more popular, says a prominent merchandising man, if housewives were not misled by the idea that they must be thawed before cooking.

Frozen meats or poultry, precooked or in the raw, can be prepared without previous thawing. Steaks, thick or thinner, and chops of all types can be cooked from the frozen state. In some instances, as with beef, taste tests have shown that cooking the meat before thawing preserves juices and flavor. A series of taste tests conducted at Columbia University and the University of Montana showed that such steaks were preferred to those which had previously been thawed.

Methods of cookery are exactly the same as usual. The cooking time is roughly twice as long. Temperatures are pretty much the same.

Frozen chicken livers and kidneys should be slightly thawed at room temperature or by plunging the package into hot water for 3 or 4 minutes. The thawing need not be, in fact should not be, complete, but just enough to separate the pieces.

In some markets packaged meats suitable for stewing are becoming increasingly popular. It is not really necessary to brown the meats beforehand. Many people believe that stews are just as tasty when this time-consuming procedure is eliminated. A dash of browning sauce gives a rich, dark color to the gravy.

If you insist on browning meat, why not place the foil package —open and unwrapped, of course—on a rack set in a broiler pan in a good hot oven, about 450° F. In 8 to 10 minutes the meat should be beautifully browned.

ALL ABOUT STEAKS

This is a subject as wide as the world or at least as broad as America. Except for the thickest of steaks, pan-broiling or grilling on a skillet is best. Of course you can use glowing charcoals, but the outdoorsy look and taste come from the air, not the charcoal. Thus, if you broil indoors, keep the door open.

The best of steaks are well aged, well marbled, or flecked with fat. The fat should be firm and flaky, cream-colored or whitish rather than yellow. Good fresh beef, which many people prefer, is bright red in color. Well-aged beef, the choice of connoisseurs, has the look of a glass of fine old Burgundy. Preferred steaks for broiling include porterhouse, sirloin, rib steaks—especially those cut from the first three ribs—shell steaks, T-bone steaks, and the filet mignon. The filet is the tenderest part of the tenderloin of beef. It is so tender, in fact, that for some people it seems to lack character. If you're buying filets for several people, it is often wiser to buy a whole piece and then cut into individual steaks from 1 to 1¼ inches thick. Less expensive cuts of meat are often tenderized and broiled exactly like other steaks.

Most steak lovers like thick steaks. For broiling, steaks should be cut at least 1½ inches thick and preferably 2 to 2½ inches thick. Do not look for a steak that has only a very little fat on it, for fat is necessary for good quality. Allow your butcher to trim away all excess fat, however, and score the edges deeply so that the steak will lie nice and flat.

First, massage your steak on all sides, including the fat, with dry mustard. The mustard does not give a mustardy taste but lends a delightful savor and crispness. Salt or pepper the steak before it goes to the broiler.

A great many people like to rub their steaks with a cut clove of garlic or sprinkle it with garlic salt. I happen to think that garlic interferes with the taste of beef, but this is personal.

Preheat the broiler. Grease the rack very well with oil or suet. Place steak on rack and put rack at least 3 inches away from the heat. For a steak that is 2 inches thick, cook about 3 minutes on the first side, turn and cook about 6 minutes on the second side. Turn again and finish for another 3 or 4 minutes. This meat will be very rare indeed. It may be too rare to suit you. To test for doneness without a thermometer, make a small cut with a sharp knife near the bone and judge for yourself.

At Serving Time:

Sprinkle both sides with salt and freshly ground black pepper. Add a good-sized pat of butter, if desired. Place on a sizzling hot platter on the hot tray. Cut in diagonal slices and place on toasty hot plates or on warmed or lightly toasted buttered French or rye bread.

TO BROIL SANS BROILER

Broiling or grilling over or under flames, glowing coals or coils, indoors or outdoors, is not the end-all and be-all of great steak cookery.

Unless your steak is quite thick, it is difficult in a broiler to achieve the crusty look on the outside and meat that is rare in the middle. Far better to pan-grill in a large heavy skillet.

Since electric skillets are so popular and comparatively little instruction is available on their proper use for pan-broiling, we have included directions for the use of thermostatic controls. If you, like us, are addicted to a heavy, old black iron "spider," just remember that 380° means hot; 325° is moderate; 275° is low.

STEAK MAXIM

When the Vaudables, Louis and Maggie, owners of Maxim's in Paris, came to dinner at our place in New York, Louis insisted that he would cook the steak. This steak was a very thick, well-aged sirloin. He insisted upon a frying pan rather than the broiler and on salt before cooking. "It is not true," he said, "that salt draws out the juices, as you Americans say. On the contrary it makes the meat crisp."

YOU WILL NEED:

1 (6-pound) sirloin steak, about 2 inches thick	Cracked peppercorns
	Salt
Butter or margarine	Armagnac or American whiskey

Cut most of the fat from steak; massage steak with a little softened butter or margarine on both sides. Press coarsely cracked black peppercorns into the meat, patting them so that they stick. If possible, allow to stand at room temperature for an hour, so that the flavor permeates.

Preheat heavy iron or electric skillet to 380° F. Rub skillet with a bit of the steak fat. Salt the meat and sear first on one side, then on the other. Turn the meat and hold it so that the fat is brown too. Turn heat down to 325° F. and cook 25 minutes altogether, about 15 minutes on one side, 10 on the other. If you are not ready to eat at this point, simply turn the heat down to 180° F. All of this is done uncovered. A cover would make it steamy.

SERVES 6 TO 8.

At Serving Time:

Remove steak to a heated platter; scrape all the little brown bits off the bottom of the skillet. Strain fat, or not, as you please. (Louis Vaudable did, we don't—we like bits in our sauce). Return juices to the skillet and add an equal quantity Armagnac (or you could use American whiskey), a small piece of butter. Heat at 275° until butter browns slightly. This is your sauce. Carve steak in thin strips and pour sauce over each portion.

Variation:

Steak Flambé

Proceed as above but omit the peppercorns and bring steak and skillet to the table. Set thermostat at 200° F. Pour on ½ cup Armagnac or bourbon. When the red light goes off, set the liquor ablaze with a match and allow the fire to blaze for a minute or two. Cover the pan for a moment in order to put out the blaze and then proceed to carve as above. Generally you will not feel the need to have extra butter.

BUDGET VERSION OF STEAK MAXIM

Survey after survey shows that steak is America's favorite meat. Yet the finest steaks are so expensive that they cannot be served as often as most of us would like. With the use of modern meat tenderizers you can broil the less expensive cuts of beef.

The meat should be cut about 2 to 3 inches thick from top or bottom round, sirloin tip, heel of round, boneless blade, or arm chuck or rump. It should weigh approximately 3 to 3¹/₂ pounds boneless, or approximately 3¹/₂ to 4 pounds with the bone in.

YOU WILL NEED:

1 (3- to 4-pound) chuck, round, rump,
    bonelsss blade or sirloin tip steak
Meat tenderizer, seasoned or
    unseasoned

Before cooking, slash the fat edges of the meat. Sprinkle all surfaces with meat tenderizer. You may use either seasoned or unseasoned tenderizer. Either takes the place of salt. Seasoned tenderizer also carries the flavor of garlic and has some paprika and herbs. Pierce all sides of the meat deeply at about 1-inch intervals with a sharp, sturdy fork.

Broil 4 to 6 inches from the source of heat. Cook 13 minutes per side for rare, or 15 minutes per side for medium.

SERVES 4 TO 6.

At Serving Time:

Cut in thin diagonal slices across the grain at approximately a 30-degree angle. Three or more slices will make a generous portion.

FAMILY STEAK AU POIVRE

This is another economical version of Steak Maxim.

Today it is possible, through the use of a powdered meat tenderizer, to achieve an extraordinarily fine steak au poivre using chuck steak or round steak. The meat should be cut about 2 to 3 inches thick from the top or bottom round. Or you could use the less expensive tip of the sirloin. Or ask for the heel of the round or boneless blade or arm chuck (some call it shoulder chuck) or a rump steak. Such a steak should weigh approximately 3 to 3¹/₂ pounds if it is boneless meat—about ¹/₂ pound more if there is a bone in it.

Before cooking, slash the edge of the fat, sprinkle all surfaces with meat tenderizer, using about as much tenderizer as you would salt. Do not add salt. Pierce all sides deeply at about 1-inch intervals with a sharp kitchen fork so that the tenderizer will penetrate.

YOU WILL NEED:

1 (3- to 4-pound) steak (see above for
   varieties)
Black peppercorns
Butter or margarine
Armagnac, cognac, or whiskey

You may use the cracked black pepper that comes ready to use in jars, but never use powdered black pepper—it will be very bitter. Or you can crack your own peppercorns in the blender. Do not use the powdery bits. Strain them out. Unless the steak is very much marbled, massage it with soft butter or olive oil. Then press in the coarsely crushed black pepper, covering all surfaces. You will need at least 2 or 3 tablespoons pepper, maybe more. Heat electric skillet to 380°. Add 1 tablespoon butter or margarine. Sear steak quickly, first on one side, then on the other, and then sear the fat side too by holding it against the hot surface. Turn thermostat to 325° and allow to cook uncovered 20 to 25 minutes. No further turning is necessary.

SERVES 4 TO 6.

At Serving Time:

Remove steak to heated platter and keep warm. Do not cover. Scrape any bits off the bottom of the pan and put with the juices through a strainer. Then return to skillet; add a couple of tablespoons of butter and 3 or 4 tablespoons of Armagnac, cognac, or bourbon whiskey. Heat together and serve this sauce over the steak. Cut in thin diagonal slices about ¹/₂-inch thick across the grain at about a 30-degree angle. You will need at least 3 or 4 slices per portion.

Variation:

Steak au Poivre Flambé

Instead of adding the brandy or whiskey to the sauce, you may warm 1/2 cup of whatever spirit you choose to about 100° F.—not anywhere close to boiling. This can be done very easily on the hot tray in a small silver or copper cup or pan. Set a match to the warm liquor and pour flaming over the meat.

STEAK DIANE

At the Quo Vadis restaurant in New York and many other places of astronomical prices and gastronomical fame, Steak Diane is a specialty. Use very thinly sliced sirloin steak. A dramatic dish to prepare at the table!

YOU WILL NEED:

2 pounds sirloin steak
3 tablespoons butter or margarine
1/4 cup onion
1/4 cup parsley
1 teaspoon prepared mustard
1/2 teaspoon pepper
1 tablespoon Worcestershire sauce
1/4 cup cognac

Have on hand 2 pounds sirloin steak cut only about 1/4- to 1/2-inch thick. Preheat electric skillet to 380° F. or even 400° F., and when the light goes off, place in the pan 1 tablespoon butter or margarine and brown steaks one at a time, very quickly. Transfer to a hot platter on a hot tray. Place in the skillet 2 more tablespoons butter; add 1/4 cup finely chopped onion. Cook only about 1 minute until the onion becomes slightly tender. Add 1/4 cup finely chopped parsley, 1 teaspoon prepared mustard, 1/2 teaspoon freshly ground black pepper, and 1 tablespoon Worcestershire sauce. Stir and allow to heat. Return the steaks to the pan, dipping each in the sauce, being sure that each one is well coated with sauce.

Slightly warm ¹/₄ cup cognac in a silver or copper saucepan or ramekin. Set fire to the cognac with a match and pour the spirit over the steaks in the skillet.

SERVES 4.

At Serving Time:

The whole operation actually occurs at serving time, but at the very moment of serving, the steaks should be aflame.

Variation:

Economical Steak Diane

Use chuck or round steak instead of sirloin. Sprinkle with meat tenderizer, using ¹/₂ teaspoon to a pound of meat. Proceed as above.

BAKED LAMB CHOPS FARCI

Because these chops need no watching while they are baking in the oven, they are a perfect choice for the hostess cook.

YOU WILL NEED:

4 to 6 thick loin lamb chops
1 package prepared poultry stuffing
Flour
1 egg, slightly beaten

Have chops cut about 1¹/₂-inches thick and slit through the lean meat right to the bone. Prepare packaged poultry stuffing according to directions, reserving about ¹/₂ cup for coating the chops. Place inside the chop as much stuffing as the space will hold. Press together lightly. Skewer with a toothpick if you wish. Dip chops in flour, slightly beaten egg, and reserved poultry stuffing. If the crumbs are coarse roll them out. Set chops in a buttered baking dish that can be taken to the table. Bake in a hot oven, 425° F., about 30 minutes, at which time the meat should be sufficiently cooked and the crumbs deliciously browned.

SERVES 3 TO 4.

At Serving Time:

Serve plain or with sauce jardinière, made by heating 1 (10½-ounce) can beef gravy with 2 tablespoons dehydrated mixed vegetable flakes. Makes 1 cup sauce—enough for 4 to 6 chops.

GRILLED RACK OF LAMB

The next time you are about to order lamb chops for 4 or 6, why not have instead an impressive rack of lamb—the same chops but all in one piece, not separated. The butcher should remove the chine (chef's word for backbone) and cut the meat away from the bones, as in the crown. Protect the bones from burning by wrapping them in aluminum foil, and roast in the oven at 325° F. or grill on a spit. It is a fallacy to believe that meats need to be boned in order to go on the spit. After all, in the rotisserie you cook a chicken or turkey complete with bones. Just be sure that the meat is properly balanced on the spit so that it cooks evenly on all sides.

YOU WILL NEED:

Rack of lamb (1 pound per person)
Garlic clove or ½ cut lemon
2 tablespoons olive oil
1 tablespoon lemon juice
½ cup dry white wine, very dry sherry,
    or Solera

Season the lamb by rubbing it well with a cut clove of garlic or ½ cut lemon and baste occasionally with the drippings, to which you should add a couple of tablespoons olive oil, 1 tablespoon lemon juice, and ½ cup dry white wine or very dry sherry. Roast in oven at 325° F. or on a spit in the rotisserie.

SERVES 4 TO 6.

At Serving Time:

Classic accompaniments for rack of lamb are dauphine potatoes and buttered carrots, heavily parsleyed. An excellent way to come by dauphine potatoes: Use frozen potato puffs, heat according to package directions, and sprinkle lightly with nutmeg.

LAMB ON SKEWERS, GRECIAN STYLE

Many long centuries ago, when brave Achilles turned the spit and Patrocles roasted onions in the fire, meat was cut into collops and speared upon skewers or sometimes swords. So the bivouac fires of warriors in the field gave rise to the shish kebab of the Near East, the shaslik of Russia, and the Greek souvlakia, the simplest and most ingeniously flavored of them all. The Greeks use no vinegar or wine, for they believe that these acids alter the true lamb taste. Sometimes lemon juice is sprinkled over the meat at the table.

YOU WILL NEED:

2 pounds lamb leg or shoulder	1/2 teaspoon pepper
1 small onion, finely chopped	2 tomatoes
1 tablespoon olive oil	Bay leaves
2 tablespoons chopped parsley	Oregano
2 teaspoons salt	Lemon juice (optional)

Cut 2 pounds of meat from leg or shoulder of lamb into pieces the size of large walnuts. Place in a bowl 1 small onion chopped fine, 1 tablespoon olive oil, 2 tablespoons chopped parsley, 2 teaspoons salt, and 1/2 teaspoon pepper; mix thoroughly. Dip meat into this mixture and roll around until well covered. Cut 2 tomatoes into quarters and the quarters into halves; place 5 to 6 pieces of meat on each skewer, alternating with tomatoes and bay leaves. Tomatoes should be pierced through the skin side so that they will not fall off. Broil about 10 minutes, turning often, and sprinkle with oregano. The bay leaves will probably begin to glow around the edges, imparting a glorious flavor to the meat far more delicate than you get when you marinate the meat for several hours with the bay leaves as the Russians do.

SERVES 4 TO 6.

At Serving Time:

Souvlakia is generally served with a tossed salad, rice pilaf, and yogurt (often flavored with fresh chopped mint or dill).

PAN-BROILED PORK CHOPS

YOU WILL NEED:

6 loin pork chops
Salt and pepper
1 tablespoon fresh or freeze-dried
   chopped parsley, rosemary, or
   oregano
$^2/_3$ cup wine

Have the pork chops cut about 1 inch thick. Sprinkle with salt and pepper. Place in a heavy greased frying pan; brown on both sides. Pour off the fat. Sprinkle with 1 tablespoon fresh or freeze-dried chopped parsley, rosemary, or oregano. Pour around the chops 1 tablespoon of wine for each chop, about $^2/_3$ cup. You may use red or white wine, Marsala, or sherry. Cover and slowly cook over low heat until tender and richly browned, about 20 minutes. If pan is well covered, the wine and the fat from the chops should keep meat from sticking. However, if liquid cooks away, add a little hot water.

SERVES 3 TO 4.

At Serving Time:

Serve with mashed potatoes, baked sweet potatoes, or saffron rice.

HAM—RED OR RED-EYE GRAVY

Though milk gravy brings a blur of gentle memories to Midwesterners, it is the red or red-eye gravy that calls forth greatest enthusiasm from

anyone with roots in the South. Red gravy can be made only by frying,
which actually means pan-broiling raw smoked ham.

YOU WILL NEED:

Raw smoked ham (1 slice per serving)
1 cup coffee (optional)
Milk or cream (optional)
Red pepper or Tabasco
Sugar (optional)
Mustard (optional)
Paprika (optional)

First rub skillet with a good piece of amber-hued ham fat, and
when the pan is fairly hot, add ham slices cut about 1/4-inch thick.
Keep turning the ham frequently as the slices cook to keep them
flat. Remove the ham from the skillet and keep it warm. Add
about 1 cup of water or coffee to the drippings in the pan or
enough to loosen the brown particles that are there. Stir and
cook until most of the water evaporates. Some people add milk
or cream—another version of milk gravy. Season to taste with a
touch of red pepper or Tabasco, a mite of sugar, maybe, and the
same of mustard, and you may add, if you wish, a speck of
paprika.

At Serving Time:

Serve gravy promptly with ham, for if the ham is allowed to
stand too long, it will harden and be tough as leather.

UNBAKED, BAKED HAM AU COGNAC

Flouting all books, all recipes, we hit on the idea of a glazed ham, what
we generally call baked ham, but without baking! We used a canned
ham which needs no cooking. A liquid benison of blazing spirit does the
glazing. Endless variations are possible. You may use honey, maple or

caramel syrup, marmalade, or preserves instead of brown sugar. Vary the seasonings to suit your mood.

The principle remains the same. Flambéed instead of heated, the meat retains all its juices. There is no drying out in the oven.

YOU WILL NEED:

1 (5-pound) canned ham
Softened butter, margarine or bacon
  drippings
Dijon mustard
Cracked black peppercorns
1/2 cup dark brown sugar or apricot
  preserves
1/2 cup toasted bread crumbs
3 bay leaves
Curl of orange peel
3/4 cup cognac, brandy, whiskey, or
  rum

Rub a 5-pound canned solid meaty ham with softened butter, margarine, or bacon drippings. Set on an attractive, heated flameproof platter. Spread top and sides with Dijon mustard. Scatter coarsely cracked black peppercorns over the top. Pat on 1/2 cup dark brown sugar, then 1/2 cup toasted bread crumbs, or spread with apricot preserves and scatter with toasted bread crumbs. Decorate with 3 bay leaves arranged rather like a *fleur-de-lys* and a curl of orange peel.

In a metal cup or small pan, warm to body heat or until it begins to give off fragrance, 3/4 cup cognac, brandy, whiskey, or rum. Set liquor aflame with kitchen match or taper. Pour burning spirit over and around the ham, then spoon it over the ham. To keep the blaze going as long as possible and make the glaze thick and glossy, set platter over heat for a few minutes so that the juices become syrupy. Keep spooning.

SERVES 20.

At Serving Time:

Serve at room temperature. Ham should be sliced wafer thin.

BAKED HAM WITH ORANGE BURGUNDY GLAZE

YOU WILL NEED:

1 ham with bone
Whole cloves
1/2 cup brown sugar, firmly packed
1 (6-ounce) can frozen orange juice,
   undiluted
1 cup Burgundy
1/2 teaspoon cinnamon
1/2 teaspoon dry mustard

Bake a ham according to packer's instructions. One hour before the end of cooking time, remove ham from oven. Drain off excess fat. Remove rind and score fat in a diamond pattern. Center each diamond with a clove. Combine 1/2 cup brown sugar, firmly packed; 1 (6-ounce) can frozen orange juice concentrate, thawed; 1 cup Burgundy; 1/2 teaspoon cinnamon; and 1/2 teaspoon dry mustard in a saucepan. Simmer, stirring, 5 minutes. Pour over ham and return to oven. Baste every 15 minutes until ham is done. If desired, serve remaining sauce in gravy boat after skimming fat from the top.

At Serving Time:

Serve with mashed potatoes, baked sweet potato, or saffron rice.

PICADILLO

A Latin-American hash of distinction.

YOU WILL NEED:

About 2 cups leftover roast beef, cut in
  tiny pieces
2 tablespoons olive oil
Salt and pepper
1 package frozen hash-brown potatoes
1 bay leaf
2 tablespoons chopped parsley
4 tablespoons white wine or white
  vinegar

Chop or cut leftover roast beef into tiny pieces. If you have 2 cups of beef you will need 3 tablespoons olive oil. Heat oil in a large skillet. Add the beef, sprinkle with salt and pepper, then add 1 package frozen hash-brown potatoes. Cook over high heat until hash begins to crisp on the bottom, about 8 minutes. Add 1 bay leaf, 2 tablespoons chopped parsley, and 4 tablespoons white wine or white vinegar. Cover and simmer about 10 minutes longer.

SERVES 3 TO 4.

At Serving Time:

Serve with a green salad or crisp carrot sticks, celery, and radishes.

FRANKFURTERS PAPRIKA

Paprika dishes are the classics of Hungary. When made with a quick-cooking meat, they are swift as well as hearty and savory.

YOU WILL NEED:

2 large onions, chopped
2 tablespoons butter or lard

1 cup hot water
1 beef bouillon cube
1 1/2 tablespoons sweet Hungarian
   paprika
1 green pepper or 2 tomatoes,
   chopped (optional)
4 frankfurters
Salt and pepper to taste
Dill or caraway seeds (optional)
Fresh dill or parsley (optional)

Cut or chop 2 large onions into small pieces and brown in 2 tablespoons butter or lard until soft; add 1 cup hot water and 1 beef bouillon cube. Sprinkle lavishly with about 1 1/2 tablespoons sweet Hungarian paprika (using at least 1 teaspoonful for each person); 1 chopped green pepper and/or 2 chopped tomatoes may be added along with the paprika. Simmer 3 or 4 minutes. Add 4 frankfurters cut into 1-inch lengths. Mix well and cook long enough to heat thoroughly, about 15 minutes. Season with salt and pepper; a few dill seeds or caraway seeds may be added if desired.

SERVES 4.

At Serving Time:

Serve with buttered noodles, rice, or mashed potatoes. Garnish if you like with green pepper rings or strips, fresh dill or parsley.

Gourmet Cooking under Pressure

There was a time not too far back when I feared, mistrusted, and generally loathed the pressure cooker, considering it a contrivance only slightly less devilish than a tommy gun and not much more closely related to gracious eating.

Like many others, I had my first introduction to pressure-cooking during World War II, when yielding to pressures of a different sort—enthusiastically, patriotically, but not too efficiently—I attempted to can a crop of green beans. For some peculiar reason still unexplained, the cooker, the jars, and the beans blew up. So, at the same time, did I. For years, as far as the pressure cooker was concerned, I stayed in a state of seethe. For years our pressure cooker was kept in dusty disuse at the back of the deepest, darkest cupboard in our house in the country.

From time to time I read about pressure-cooking. I delved at times into recipe booklets and even books but nothing kindled my interest. Far more depressing than the literature were certain soupy, generally soggy and soppy vegetables and stews served to me on various occasions and usually by someone in the mood for saving something—either time or effort or fuel or vitamins.

Then a distinguished gourmet friend, Ann Williams-Heller, offered to share with me a recipe for Hungarian goulash that had won her a thousand-dollar prize. This was, without doubt, the most perfectly balanced, the most knowingly seasoned, the most authentically Magyar goulash I have ever encountered, and it called for a pressure cooker. Unconvinced, I tried the recipe two ways. First I simmered it on top of the stove in the traditional fashion and then I tried it her way under pressure in one-fourth the time. The pressure-cooked goulash was, in the opinion of all who tasted it, equal, and in certain subtle ways, even a little better, richer, more "married."

HUNGARIAN BEEF GOULASH

This recipe, with some slight personal variations of my own, was invented by Ann Williams-Heller. It is a prize-winning recipe that changed my whole attitude toward the pressure cooker.

YOU WILL NEED:

2 pounds stewing beef, cubed
1/2 cup flour
1 tablespoon lard or fat
1 can condensed onion soup or 1
    package dehydrated onion-soup mix
    plus 2 cups water

1 tablespoon sweet Hungarian paprika
1 tablespoon vinegar
1 tablespoon caraway seeds
1 teaspoon marjoram
1 teaspoon capers
2 bay leaves
2 sprigs parsley
1/4 cup dry sherry (optional)

In a paper bag with 1/2 cup flour, shake 2 pounds stewing beef, which has been cut into 1- or 1 1/2-inch cubes. The meat should be evenly covered with flour. Brown the meat in 1 tablespoon lard or cooking fat, turning occasionally. You can do this in the pressure cooker at about 380° F. Add 1 can condensed onion soup or 1 package dehydrated onion-soup mix and 2 cups water, 1 tablespoon sweet Hungarian paprika, 1 tablespoon vinegar, 1 tablespoon caraway seeds, 1 teaspoon marjoram, 1 teaspoon capers, 2 bay leaves, 2 sprigs parsley, and 1/4 cup dry sherry if you want it. Cook under 15-pound pressure 15 minutes for 1-inch cubes or 20 minutes for 1 1/2-inch cubes. Bring pressure down immediately and allow to simmer very gently at 180° to 200° F. until meltingly tender, or as long as you please.

SERVES 6.

At Serving Time:
Serve with broad noodles or boiled potatoes.

CORNED BEEF AND CABBAGE

Some corned beef requires soaking, some doesn't. Ask the man who sells it to you. If it needs soaking, an hour or maybe a little more should be sufficient. The corned beef that comes packed in a plastic bag with a liquid surrounding it is usually ready-to-cook without soaking. If you want to slice the beef for sandwiches, you can tie it with string to keep it in shape.

YOU WILL NEED:

1 (4-pound) corned beef brisket
1/2 bay leaf
4 peppercorns
7 small onions
3 whole cloves
7 carrots
1 teaspoon celery flakes or 1 small stalk
    celery
1 small head cabbage
Parsley butter (optional)

Place meat in pressure cooker, add 2 cups cold water, 1/2 bay leaf, 4 peppercorns, 1 small onion cut in pieces, 3 whole cloves, 1 carrot cut in slices, 1 teaspoon celery flakes or a small stalk celery cut into pieces. Adjust cover. Set thermostat to 400° until steam comes up steadily. Cook at 15 pounds pressure for 1 hour, Reduce pressure immediately by letting cold water run down the side. When pressure is completely down, remove cover; add 6 small onions, 6 small carrots cut crosswise in half, and 1 small head cabbage cut into 6 or 8 wedges. Cook uncovered 10 to 15 minutes longer, until cabbage is tender.

SERVES 6 TO 8.

At Serving Time:

Serve the beef on a platter surrounded by vegetables. A little melted butter with or without chopped parsley may be poured over the vegetables. Have on hand a pot of sharp mustard and/or horseradish sauce.

THE WORLD'S EASIEST STEW

In the freezer and on the shelf the ingredients for making this stew can be kept always on hand. This has been a lifesaver to us when we go to the country on winter weekends.

YOU WILL NEED:

1 tablespoon shortening
2 pounds fresh or frozen stewing beef,
   cubed
1 package dehydrated onion-soup mix

Heat your pressure cooker to 300° F. When the light goes off, add 1 tablespoon shortening and brown 2 pounds beef cut into cubes for stew. If frozen, the meat need not be thawed. The browning will take longer if meat is frozen, of course, but what you desire will be swiftly accomplished. Keep turning and moving the meat around so that all surfaces are exposed to heat.

When meat is brown, add the contents of 1 package dehydrated onion-soup mix. This supplies not only the onions but also all the seasoning necessary. Now add 1 to 2 cups water, depending upon the size of the pan. Cover and cook under pressure, according to manufacturer's directions, 15 minutes. Bring pressure down immediately by letting cold water run down the side of the pot. Remove top and replace so that a little air gets into the stew. Simmer about half an hour longer. Even if allowed to stand over low heat for several hours, the meat will not dry out, the liquid will not boil away, and the stew will take on the most melting quality.

SERVES 4 TO 6.

At Serving Time:

Serve with boiled potatoes, rice, cornmeal mush, barley, or any other starchy vegetable desired.

Variation:

Beef Stew with Carrots

After removing stew from pressure cooker add 1 cup carrots cut into 1/2-inch chunks, and cook until carrots are tender or as much longer as you like. Quartered potatoes may be added to the stew along with the carrots, or better still, cook them separately.

Vegetables with a Difference

Standbys of the hurried cook are canned and quick-frozen vegetables. Both can, when properly prepared, retain a great deal of the flavor, color, and vitamin value of garden-fresh vegetables. On the other hand, they can be, and very frequently are, ruined by carelessness—too much water, overcooking.

Quick-frozen vegetables are best when they are not allowed to thaw before cooking but are simply placed as a solid-frozen block in a small amount of rapidly boiling water. They should be allowed to cook uncovered over a moderate heat until completely thawed all the way through, at which time the water should be boiling in the center as well as around the edge of the pan. You may hurry this process along by breaking the block with a fork and turning the vegetable from time to time. But do this carefully so as not to destroy the shape of the vegetable. After the water is boiling, turn down the heat, cover the pan, and cook until just barely tender. Package directions will give you the approximate cooking time for each vegetable. When in doubt, cook less rather than longer than advised.

Why not turn to the French technique of heating vegetables in butter? Melt butter or margarine in a heavy frying pan or saucepan but do not brown. Place the vegetables (canned, fresh, cooked or frozen) in the butter, and heat.

Seasoning Chart for Frozen Vegetables

The ancients believed that herbs were most effective when picked under the signs of their respective plants. But modern homemakers know that herbs, whether freshly picked or dried, are a little treasury to draw on for giving variety and excitement to everyday foods.

The art of seasoning is neither difficult nor mysterious when you follow a few fundamental rules. Remember that herbs should heighten but never disguise the flavor of the dish. Dried herbs are about four times as strong as fresh ones; 1/2 teaspoon of the dried product is equivalent to 2 scant teaspoons fresh. To bring out the aromatic oils lurking in the leaves or seeds, chop fresh herbs or powder dried ones before using.

Herb cookery with frozen foods constitutes a new branch of an age-old art. Since many frozen prepared dishes are already seasoned, additional herbs are used primarily for a note of individuality, or to transform the dish. For example, the addition of curry powder, cinnamon, and perhaps some saffron to frozen creamed chicken or frozen chicken à la king turns them into quick chicken curry.

Yet many frozen products—particularly unsauced frozen vegetables are not seasoned, and herbs may be added with (controlled) abandon. If you usually place a pat of butter or margarine on vegetables, try creaming the butter first with one of these herbs, then let the herb butter melt over the hot vegetables.

In addition to salt and pepper, you might try the following combinations:

Asparagus: nutmeg, curry or turmeric, sesame seeds
Green beans: marjoram, rosemary, sesame, tarragon, garlic, dill seed
Lima beans: nutmeg, marjoram, sage
Broccoli: oregano, celery seed

Brussels sprouts: garlic, sesame seed
Carrots: ginger, cinnamon, parsley, tarragon, celery seed, mint
Cauliflower: nutmeg, mustard, parsley, poppy seed, rosemary, sesame seed, paprika
Corn: chives, oregano, parsley
Green peas: chives, mint, sweet basil, nutmeg, ginger
Potatoes: paprika, chives, dill, oregano, sweet basil, thyme
Spinach: nutmeg, garlic, marjoram
Yellow squash: ginger, cinnamon, nutmeg, cloves
Zucchini squash: caraway seed, garlic, oregano, parsley, poppy seed, rosemary

Cooking Frozen Foods en Papillote

En papillote, or paper-bag cookery, has been used for centuries by chefs as one of the best methods of retaining the natural flavor, aroma, and juices of meat, poultry, fish, and vegetables. En papillote, French for "in cocoon," in cooking terms is simply baking food in a paper case. Purists, of course, insist on using vegetable parchment paper, but modernists find aluminum foil more convenient and equally good. And foil, being fireproof, has the added advantage of being usable over an open fire such as a charcoal grill.

Frozen foods are another product of the twentieth century to take to outdoor cooking. Frozen vegetables, for instance, can be wrapped in foil packets and cooked along with other foods over the charcoal grill. No pots and pans are needed—just a sheet of heavy aluminum foil or two sheets of regular foil large enough to wrap the contents of each package of frozen vegetables.

Lay a pat of butter or margarine on the foil; over it place the still-frozen vegetables. Top with a second pat of butter and sprinkle with salt, pepper, and seasonings. (Or use frozen sauced vegetables and omit butter, salt, and pepper.) Seal the packet all around with double folds, allowing some room for expansion of steam.

AMAZING ASPARAGUS

Never again will your asparagus go limp with the color of khaki, no matter how many traffic jams your folks encounter or how long they linger over cocktails. This method, though it sounds wilder than wild, makes and keeps asparagus or broccoli garden-green, crisp, and unbelievably fresh-tasting.

Clean and scrape fresh asparagus and cut off ends evenly. Place 3 layers deep in a heavy, shallow cook-and-serve dish. Cover completely with cold water to stand 1/2 inch above the asparagus. Add 1/2 teaspoon each salt and sugar (does miracles). Bring to boil uncovered. Cook, still uncovered, 2 to 3 minutes. Off-heat, let stand still uncovered at least 8 minutes or until ready to serve. The vegetable continues to cook as it cools, but won't overcook— there's a built-in thermostat. If the asparagus gets stone-cold, simply reheat and serve promptly.

Be superelegant—remove stalks from water with slotted spoon. Dry on paper towel.

OPEN-FACED ASPARAGUS BENEDICT

YOU WILL NEED:

2 (9-ounce) packages frozen asparagus
   (cuts and tips) in hollandaise sauce
2 English muffins, split and toasted
2 hard-cooked eggs, sliced

Heat 2 (9-ounce) packages frozen asparagus (cuts and tips) hollandaise-style by submerging frozen pouches in boiling water as packages direct. Meanwhile, split 2 English muffins and toast lightly. Spoon hot asparagus with sauce over muffin halves and garnish with slices of hard-cooked eggs.

SERVES 4.

ASPARAGUS WITH EGGS PARMESAN

A vegetable entrée with an honorable and ancient Italian lineage, perfect for luncheon. Canned green asparagus or quick-frozen stalks make it with ease and speed.

YOU WILL NEED:

1 can asparagus tips or 1 package
   quick-frozen asparagus
Butter or margarine
4 to 6 eggs
Salt and pepper to taste
1/2 cup grated Parmesan cheese
Paprika or parsley
1 lemon, quartered (optional)

Drain canned asparagus tips or cook 1 package quick-frozen asparagus. Asparagus cuts may be used but the dish will then look less attractive. Arrange the cooked asparagus in 4 individual baking dishes or 1 shallow baking dish that can be brought to the table. The baking dish should be generously oiled or buttered. On top of the asparagus break 4 to 6 eggs. Season with salt and pepper. Sprinkle with 1/2 cup grated Parmesan cheese. Set in moderate oven at 325° until eggs are set, about 8 to 10 minutes.

SERVES 4.

At Serving Time:

Garnish with a flicker of paprika or bit of parsley and provide if you wish small sections of lemon to be squeezed over the eggs.

ARTICHOKE ARTISTRY

The artichoke is one vegetable that takes most kindly to pressure-cooking. Choose smooth, dark-green, tightly closed heads that are not too big. Wash them carefully. Cut the stem close to the leaves. If the tops are dry and prickly, cut them down with scissors or a long, sharp knife on a carving board. Actually, if the artichokes are fresh and not too mature, there is no reason why you should have to do anything more than wash and remove part of the stems. With pressure-cooking, tying is unnecessary. The artichokes will keep their shape.

YOU WILL NEED:

Artichokes (1 per serving)
2 tablespoons lemon juice or vinegar
1/2 teaspoon salt
Melted butter or margarine

Place artichokes in the pressure cooker along with 1 cup water, 2 tablespoons lemon juice or vinegar, and 1/2 teaspoon salt. Cook 10 minutes at 15 pounds pressure. Reduce pressure immediately. Test artichokes for doneness by pulling off a leaf and seeing if it is tender. If not, continue cooking, uncovered, a few minutes.

At Serving Time:

Serve hot with melted butter or margarine, flavored if you like with lemon juice and parsley or with Hollandaise Sauce (page 152), Sauce Béarnaise (page 154), or Vinaigrette Sauce (page 154).

Variation:

Italian Artichokes

Instead of lemon juice in the above recipe, use 2 tablespoons olive oil in the water, 1 clove garlic, a sprig of parsley, and serve the liquid from the pressure cooker as a sauce, removing garlic and parsley.

ARTICHOKES SANS PRESSURE

Prepare artichokes as described above. To shorten cooking time and make serving easier, remove the core, known as the "choke," with a sharp knife or a grapefruit corer. If the heads do not feel firm and tightly packed, you may want to tie a string around the artichokes to keep them in shape. Set artichokes, heads up, close together in a deepish pan and cover with boiling, salted, acidulated water, i.e., 1 tablespoon white vinegar or lemon juice added to 1 quart water. Cook covered or uncovered: Suit yourself. With core removed, artichokes should be ready in 20 or 25 minutes. Covering cuts down the time but dulls the color.

ARTICHOKE HEARTS ITALIENNE

YOU WILL NEED:

2 packages frozen artichoke hearts
1/2 cup bottled Italian-style salad
   dressing

Prepare 2 packages frozen artichoke hearts according to package directions. Heat 1/2 cup bottled Italian-style salad dressing over low heat in separate pan. Pour hot salad dressing over cooked artichoke hearts.

SERVES 6.

At Serving Time:

Sprinkle with chopped herbs (optional).

CORN PUFFS

These are the most delicate of corn fritters. They contain no flour whatsoever and no baking powder. They are troublesome only in one respect: It is hard to make enough.

YOU WILL NEED:

1 package frozen corn, cooked,
   drained, and slightly chopped
3 eggs, separated
1 teaspoon sugar
1/2 teaspoon salt
Syrup or honey

Add 1 package lightly cooked, drained, and slightly chopped frozen corn to 3 well-beaten egg yolks seasoned with 1 teaspoon sugar and 1/2 teaspoon salt. Fold in stiffly beaten whites of 3 eggs and drop by tablespoonfuls onto a hot, well-greased griddle. Turn only once when the cake begins to look dry.

MAKES ABOUT 24 PUFFS.

At Serving Time:

Serve immediately plain, or with syrup or honey.

SHOE-PEG CORN

This is a very special type of corn; the kernels are very small, shaped like the pegs that old-time cobblers used. Shoe-peg corn has recently become available frozen as well as canned. Cook according to package directions but add 1/2 teaspoon honey to the water.

YOU WILL NEED:

1 can or 1 package frozen shoe-peg corn
1/2 teaspoon honey
Freshly ground black pepper

SERVES 2 TO 4.

At Serving Time:

Sprinkle with freshly ground black pepper.

CORN ON THE COB—WILD NEW WAY

Gone are the days when it was, as Mark Twain wrote, absolutely obligatory to have a huge kettle of water billowing on the stove before you grabbed up your sunbonnet and ran out to pick the roasting ears in the Back Forty. Now the password is *cool it.* Always buy corn from markets that keep it refrigerated.

Never, never husk corn ahead of time and allow it to sit around. To enjoy the best flavor and add drama to your presentation, leave some of the husks on the cob—removing the silk, of course. At least an hour before cooking, plunge the corn into a kettle full of snow-cold water. Do not add salt, for it tends to harden the kernels. At cooking time add a little sugar or honey and lemon juice (about a tablespoon each for each gallon of water). The water should stand about two inches above the corn. Bring uncovered to a full boil and cook only one or two minutes, depending on the size and age of the corn. Off heat, let the kettle stand uncovered about 10 minutes, or until ready to serve. There is much to be said in favor of this method. The husks are not only pretty and "talkable" at the table, but they also deepen the corn flavor and help to keep the ears warm.

NEW WAY WITHOUT HUSKS

Ultraconservatives, of course, may remove husks from corn on the cob. Some of it, unfortunately, comes that way from the market. Use the same *cold*-water-plus-sugar-plus-lemon-juice method. If corn must stand and wait after cooking, it fares much better in the cooking water. Don't worry! The corn will not dry out or overcook. Water keeps cooling gradually. If necessary, you may reheat quickly just to boiling—not a second longer. Then serve immediately.

FROZEN CORN ON THE COB

Use the same technique as above. This cold-water method is the only one that insures against a cold cob covered with overdone corn kernels.

SPICED SCALLOPED TOMATOES WITH HERBS

Old-fashioned favorites like this should not be tampered with. Although this recipe uses canned tomatoes and baker's bread, the flavor is the traditional one.

YOU WILL NEED:

Butter or margarine
Bread crumbs
2 1/2 cups canned tomatoes
1 tablespoon finely chopped onion or
  dried onion flakes
1 tablespoon brown sugar
1/2 teaspoon powdered allspice
Salt and freshly ground black pepper
Toast squares

Butter a casserole and sprinkle with bread crumbs. Pour in 1 no. 2 can (about 2 1/2 cups) solidly packed canned tomatoes, 1 tablespoon finely chopped onion or dried onion flakes, 1 tablespoon brown sugar, 1/2 teaspoon powdered allspice, salt and freshly ground black pepper to taste. Cover top with 1-inch squares of buttered toast. Bake in a hot oven, 400° F., until thoroughly heated all the way through and golden brown on top, about 20 to 25 minutes.

SERVES 6.

At Serving Time:

Serve from baking dish.

Variation:

Glazed Scalloped Tomatoes

Omit allspice from the seasonings; add 4 tablespoons dark-brown sugar to the tomatoes and scatter sugar on top of toast. Dot with bits of butter. The casserole will then acquire a delicious glaze.

CORN-STUFFED TOMATOES

This is a different and interesting luncheon dish!

YOU WILL NEED:

6 good-sized tomatoes
Salt and pepper
2 cups cooked corn kernels
    (fresh, canned, or frozen)
1 egg, beaten
6 tablespoons heavy cream or
    evaporated milk
1 teaspoon sugar
1/2 teaspoon paprika
3/4 cup bread crumbs
3 tablespoons melted butter or
    margarine
Rounds of toast

Use 6 firm, good-sized tomatoes. Wash and wipe, but do not peel. Cut off tops, scoop out centers, and sprinkle with a little salt and pepper. Meanwhile, combine 2 cups cooked corn kernels with 1 beaten egg, 6 tablespoons heavy cream or evaporated milk, 1 teaspoon sugar, and 1/2 teaspoon paprika. Fill the tomatoes with this mixture, and sprinkle the tops with buttered bread crumbs (stir 3 tablespoons melted butter into 3/4 cup bread crumbs), using about 2 tablespoons buttered bread crumbs on each tomato. Bake at 375° F. about 30 minutes.

SERVES 6.

At Serving Time:

Serve plain or on rounds of toast with or without a cheese sauce.

EGGPLANT IMAM BAYELDI

Literally translated, Imam Bayeldi *means, "the Imam fainted." In the Middle East they tell this story: Imam, a prominent Muslim, was very fond of eggplant cooked with meat. But his dear wife, being a lady who liked to play the Middle Eastern version of bridge in the afternoon, forgot to go to the butcher store until it was too late. However, she had a few vegetables in the house and with these she created a dish for her lord and master, a dish with an aroma and flavor so heavenly that Imam swooned with delight. That's why the dish is called Imam Bayeldi—it is the most delicious of all vegetable dinners.*

YOU WILL NEED:

1 eggplant
$1/2$ cup olive or salad oil
2 onions, sliced
1 large green pepper, chopped
1 cup canned tomatoes
$1/4$ cup chopped parsley
Salt and pepper to taste
Cut a large-sized eggplant into quarters. Salt and allow pieces to stand until tiny drops of dark juice appear on the pieces. Meanwhile, brown gently in $1/2$ cup olive oil or salad oil 2 sliced onions, and 1 large chopped green pepper. When the vegetables are tender add 1 cup drained solid-packed canned tomatoes, $1/4$ cup chopped parsley, and salt and pepper to taste. Cook mixture about 2 minutes. Wash eggplant. Make a slit down the center of each quarter and stuff with the cooked vegetable combination. Place the quarters in a baking dish, pour a cup of water in the bottom to keep the eggplant from burning, and bake in a moderate oven, 325° F., about 40 minutes.

SERVES 2.

At Serving Time:

Serve as entrée vegetable; or chill, slice, and serve as an appetizer or a salad.

GOLDEN SQUASH WITH PECANS

YOU WILL NEED:

2 (10-ounce) packages frozen cooked
   squash or pumpkin
1/2 cup chopped pecans
1/4 cup butter or margarine
1 teaspoon cinnamon
6 tablespoons brown sugar

Cook 2 (10-ounce) packages frozen cooked squash or pumpkin according to directions. Place in a shallow casserole. Meanwhile, sauté 1/2 cup chopped pecans in 1/4 cup butter or margarine. Sprinkle nuts over squash. Mix 1 teaspoon cinnamon with 6 tablespoons brown sugar and spread over nuts. Bake uncovered in a moderate 350° F. oven 15 minutes.

SERVES 6.

At Serving Time:

Serve hot from oven in casserole in which squash was baked.

GRILLED SUCCOTASH

This recipe is good for outdoor cooking.

YOU WILL NEED:

1 package frozen succotash
Pimiento strips
Butter
Salt and pepper

On top of 1 block of frozen succotash, lay several strips canned pimiento. Dot with butter, salt, and pepper; wrap in foil. Grill about 6 minutes, turning once.

SERVES 3 TO 4.

RUSSIAN SCALLIONS

This is the perfect accompaniment to serve with a broiled lamb chop, or try it with Russian Bitki.

YOU WILL NEED:

1 bunch scallions with tops
1 cup apple cider vinegar
1 teaspoon sugar
1/4 teaspoon salt
1/4 teaspoon freshly ground black
    pepper

Cut the scallions into 1/2-inch pieces. Mix 1 cup apple cider vinegar with 1 teaspoon sugar, 1/4 teaspoon each salt and freshly ground pepper.

SERVES 6 TO 8.

At Serving Time:

Pour vinegar dressing on onions.

ZUCCHINI NEAPOLITAN

YOU WILL NEED:

2 (10-ounce) packages frozen zucchini
1 clove garlic, sliced
1 tablespoon olive oil
1 large tomato, peeled and quartered
1 1/2 teaspoons salt
1/4 teaspoon pepper
1/2 teaspoon oregano

Defrost 2 (10-ounce) packages frozen zucchini. Sauté a sliced clove of garlic in 1 tablespoon olive oil for 1 minute in a 1 1/2-quart pan. Stir in zucchini; 1 large tomato, peeled and quartered; 1 1/2 teaspoons salt; 1/4 teaspoon pepper; and 1/2 teaspoon oregano. Cover and cook over low heat 10 to 12 minutes.

SERVES 4.

PASHA BEANS

This dish utilizes leftover lamb or hot dogs. Tasty enough to please even an Oriental pasha.

YOU WILL NEED:

3 tablespoons olive or peanut oil
3 medium-sized onions, chopped
1 cup diced leftover cooked lamb or
    thinly sliced frankfurters
1 package frozen French-style green
    beans
1/2 cup bouillon or hot water with 1
    bouillon cube
2 tomatoes, peeled and thickly sliced
Salt and pepper
Nutmeg
Clove

Heat 3 tablespoons olive or peanut oil in a skillet, add 3 medium-sized, finely chopped onions and 1 cup leftover cooked lamb cut into small pieces, or you could use thinly sliced frankfurters. Stir over low heat until onion is golden brown, about 10 minutes. Add 1 package frozen French-style green beans and 1/2 cup bouillon or 1/2 cup hot water and 1 bouillon cube. Cook until the beans are wilted, i.e., 5 minutes. Arrange 2 thickly sliced, peeled tomatoes on top of the beans, cover tightly, and simmer about 10 minutes longer. Season to taste with salt, pepper, a dash nutmeg, and a few grains ground clove.

SERVES 6.

At Serving Time:

Serve as an entrée with rice and a salad.

GRILLED VEGETABLES

Excellent for broiling are halved or thickly sliced tomatoes, sliced eggplant with or without the peel, thickly sliced potatoes, and wedges or thick slices of zucchini or carrots.

YOU WILL NEED:

Fresh or parboiled vegetables
Salad oil, butter, or margarine
Salt and pepper

Brush the vegetables with salad oil, melted butter, or margarine, and season with salt and pepper. Broil until tender and lightly brown.

At Serving Time:

Serve piping hot, and if desired sprinkle with appropriate herbs. Try finely chopped basil or oregano on the tomatoes, parsley or chives on the potatoes, chopped mint on the carrots.

CARROTS VICHY

This is a vegetable dish that you will serve at your proudest little dinners. Don't be surprised if your guests ask for 2 or 3 helpings.

YOU WILL NEED:

6 large or 12 small carrots, sliced
   lengthwise
$1/2$ teaspoon salt
$1/4$ teaspoon pepper
$1/4$ teaspoon nutmeg
3 tablespoons butter or margarine
Chopped parsley

Slice 6 good-sized carrots or 12 small carrots lengthwise. Pour water into skillet or saucepan $1/4$ inch deep. Add carrots, $1/2$ teaspoon salt, $1/4$ teaspoon pepper, $1/4$ teaspoon nutmeg, and 3 tablespoons butter or margarine. Cover tightly and heat at 350° F. until the water boils, then turn down the heat to 250° F. and cook 10 minutes or until crisp-tender.

SERVES 6.

At Serving Time:

Sprinkle chopped parsley over the carrots.

BOSTON BAKED BEANS GONE TO HEAVEN

Several brands of baked beans with molasses are excellent. Only a little dressing-up is needed to give them the appearance as well as the flavor of those beans that are the pride of Boston. If you have no bean pot serve them from a casserole.

YOU WILL NEED:

2 (10³/4-ounce) cans baked beans with
    pork and molasses
1 medium onion
¹/₂ teaspoon dry mustard
¹/₂ cup dark molasses
6 strips bacon or small piece salt pork

Place 2 cans Boston baked beans in a bean pot or casserole along with 1 medium-sized whole onion, peeled, ¹/₂ teaspoon dry mustard, and ¹/₂ cup dark molasses. Cover with 6 strips bacon or small piece salt pork. Set in a moderate oven at 350° and bake 30 to 40 minutes until the beans are piping hot and bubbly, and the bacon is crisp and brown.

SERVES 6.

At Serving Time:

Serve from bean pot along with sliced and heated canned Boston brown bread, coleslaw, sliced tomatoes, and dill pickles.

ESCAROLE OR SPINACH WITH PINE NUTS

Something different in the way of a vegetable is not too easy to come by. This one has great distinction—a classical Italian background. A dramatic dish to prepare on stage in an electric skillet.

YOU WILL NEED:

6 bunches escarole or spinach (about 2
   pounds)
1/2 cup olive oil
1 large clove garlic, crushed
1/3 cup pine nuts
1/4 cup capers
1/3 cup raisins
12 Italian black olives, pitted
1 teaspoon salt
1/2 teaspoon freshly ground black
   pepper

Use 6 bunches escarole or spinach (about 2 pounds) and cut in pieces about 2 inches long, using both the outside and inside leaves. Heat 1/2 cup olive oil in a deep, heavy skillet. Add 1 large clove of garlic, crushed, 1/3 cup pine nuts, 1/4 cup capers, 1/3 cup raisins, and about 12 Italian olives, pitted. Cook 2 minutes. Add the escarole, which has been cut up in 2-inch pieces, washed, and well drained. Turn heat to low (about 275°). Cook about 15 minutes or until just tender. Add 1 teaspoon salt and 1/2 teaspoon freshly ground black pepper.

SERVES 6.

At Serving Time:

Chopped black olives and extra capers are often passed along with this vegetable.

Variation:

Instead of escarole in the above recipe, you may substitute 2 (12-ounce) packages frozen leaf spinach. Cook according to package directions. Drain carefully and proceed as above.

BROCCOLI AU GRATIN

This is a particularly good recipe for leftover broccoli.

YOU WILL NEED:

2 cups quick-frozen broccoli in stalks
   or pieces
1 (10³/4-ounce) can condensed cream
   of celery soup
¹/4 cup grated cheese (any kind—
   Cheddar is excellent)
¹/4 cup bread crumbs

Combine 2 cups lightly cooked broccoli with 1 can condensed undiluted cream of celery soup. Place in shallow baking dish. Sprinkle with ¹/4 cup each grated cheese and bread crumbs. Bake in a moderate oven at 350° F. for 15 or 20 minutes until hot and lightly brown.

SERVES 4 TO 5.

At Serving Time:

Serve from the baking dish. Good for luncheon along with grilled tomatoes and raw carrot strips.

LIMA BEANS PRINTEMPS

YOU WILL NEED:

4 scallions
2 stalks celery
2 tablespoons butter
   or margarine
2 packages frozen lima beans
   in cheese sauce

Salt and freshly ground
   black pepper
1 tablespoon lemon juice
1 tablespoon minced parsley

Wash 4 scallions and cut in 1-inch slices; wash 2 stalks celery and cut lengthwise in 1-inch pieces. Cook both vegetables slowly in 2 tablespoons butter or margarine for 10 minutes. Cook 2 packages frozen lima beans in cheese sauce according to directions and add to scallion-and-celery mixture. Add salt and freshly ground black pepper to taste, 1 tablespoon lemon juice, and 1 tablespoon minced parsley, and serve at once.

SERVES 4.

SWEET AND SOUR GREEN BEANS

YOU WILL NEED:

1 package frozen French-style green beans	1 teaspoon flour
Consommé	2 teaspoons brown sugar
1 teaspoon butter	2 teaspoons vinegar or lemon juice
	Tabasco sauce (optional)

Cook 1 package frozen French-style green beans according to package directions but using consommé instead of water. Cook beans until tender and drain. Be sure to save the broth. You should have ½ cup. Thicken this broth with 1 teaspoon butter kneaded together with 1 teaspoon flour. Season with 2 teaspoons brown sugar and 2 teaspoons vinegar or lemon juice. Add a drop of Tabasco sauce, if desired.

SERVES 4.

At Serving Time:

Reheat the beans in the sauce. Especially good with ham or pork.

POMMES MOUSSELINE

To 2 cups mashed potatoes prepared according to package directions, add ½ cup heated cream—light or heavy. Beat with rotary beater until very light and foamy.

SERVES 4.

POTATOES HAUT-BRION

(Haut-Brion is a Frenchified version of just plain old-fashioned O'Brien.)

YOU WILL NEED:

1 package frozen French-fried
   potatoes
1 large onion, sliced
Butter or salad oil
2 whole pimientos, canned, cut into
   julienne strips
2 tablespoons finely chopped parsley

Heat 1 package frozen French-fried potatoes. Keep warm, uncovered. Sauté 1 large, thinly sliced onion in butter or salad oil until golden brown. Add 2 drained canned pimientos cut into julienne strips and 2 tablespoons finely chopped parsley. Allow to heat thoroughly and sprinkle over heated French-fried potatoes.

SERVES 3 TO 4.

At Serving Time:

Serve immediately.

HEATING FROZEN FRENCH FRIES
(Cold-Start Method)

Place frozen French-fried potatoes in a single layer in a large skillet. Pour in just enough vegetable oil to cover and stir until pieces are coated. Turn heat to medium high, or if you are using a thermostat control or an electric skillet, set it at 350° F. to 375° F. (Thermostats do vary, you know.) Stir occasionally to keep the potatoes separated. Cook 12 to 13 minutes, depending upon the degree of browness desired. Turn off heat. Remove potatoes with slotted spoon. Drain on paper towels. Sprinkle with salt and coarsely ground black pepper if desired.

SWEET POTATOES WITH ORANGE GLAZE

YOU WILL NEED:

1 package frozen sweet potatoes
3 tablespoons melted butter or
   margarine
3 tablespoons orange juice
3 tablespoons brown sugar

Heat 1 package frozen sweet potatoes, which have been defrosted and drained, in a glaze made by heating together 3 tablespoons each melted butter or margarine, orange juice, and brown sugar. Shake potatoes over high heat until they glisten and glow.

SERVES 3.

GLAZED YAMS

YOU WILL NEED:

1 package frozen yams or halved sweet
   potatoes
2 tablespoons butter or margarine
$\frac{1}{2}$ teaspoon salt
Nutmeg
$\frac{1}{4}$ cup honey or maple syrup

Heat 1 package frozen yams or sweet potatoes cut in halves in syrup. Drain. Brush with 2 tablespoons melted butter or margarine, sprinkle lightly with $\frac{1}{2}$ teaspoon salt and a few grains nutmeg. Place in a buttered baking dish. Dribble $\frac{1}{4}$ cup honey or maple syrup over the yams and broil for just about 2 minutes.

SERVES 3 TO 4.

SWEET POTATOES PRALINE

YOU WILL NEED:

1 (12-ounce) package frozen candied
   sweet potatoes or yams
1 tablespoon frozen concentrated
   orange juice
1 tablespoon butter or margarine
Pralines or peanut brittle
4 tablespoons rum or bourbon
   (optional)

Heat a 12-ounce package frozen candied sweet potatoes or yams
according to package directions (some directions recommend
oven-heating and others indicate that either top-stove or oven-
heating may be done).

Ten minutes before serving, transfer sweet potatoes to casserole and sprinkle with 1 tablespoon frozen concentrated orange
juice, then dot with 1 tablespoon butter or margarine. Sprinkle
with bits of pralines or peanut brittle and place in moderate oven
(350° F.) for 10 minutes or until lightly browned.

SERVES 3 TO 4.

At Serving Time:

For extra drama slightly heat 4 tablespoons rum or bourbon. Set
alight and pour flaming over the dish. Serve flaming.

CRUSTY POTATO PANCAKES

*There was a time when potato pancakes brought visions of knuckles
grated along with the raw potatoes. The new packaged or quick-frozen
mixes make grating unnecessary, but the mixes can stand extra
seasoning.*

YOU WILL NEED:

1 (7-ounce) package potato-pancake
   mix

1 small onion, finely chopped
Milk or light cream
Cooking oil or shortening

Make up batter for potato pancakes according to package directions, but to enrich the flavor use thin cream or milk instead of water and add 1 small-sized onion, very finely chopped. For a crisp crust drop by tablespoonfuls into hot shortening or oil, which stands at least 1-inch deep in the frying pan. Fry on one side, then the other. Drain on paper towels.

SERVES 3 OR 4.

At Serving Time:

Serve with applesauce and crisp bacon or frizzled ham for late Sunday breakfast or for luncheon. Potato pancakes are traditional with sauerbraten or goulash.

FRENCH-FRIED ONIONS

With steak, grilled hamburgers, or liver, as a garnish for creamed dishes, or as an appetizer to serve between meals with cocktails or beer, nothing could be finer than French-fried onions. Try the canned variety dressed up in this manner.

YOU WILL NEED:

1 can French-fried onions (or 1
  package frozen)
Olive oil
Cayenne or freshly ground black
  pepper

Empty a can of French-fried onions into a shallow oiled pan. Brush lightly with olive oil. Sprinkle with a few grains cayenne or freshly ground black pepper. Heat in a moderate oven, 350° F., about 5 minutes.

SERVES 2 TO 4.

At Serving Time:

Serve very hot, preferably from the same pan in which they were heated.

MUSHROOMS IN CREAM UNDER GLASS

The French phrase for serving foods under glass is sous cloche *or "under a bell," and you can get glass covers at specialty shops or department stores. However, heatproof glass custard cups answer the purpose admirably and look very pretty too.*

YOU WILL NEED:

About 32 whole mushroom caps
1/4 cup butter or margarine
1 tablespoon lemon juice
1/2 teaspoon salt
Pinch pepper
1 tablespoon chopped parsley
Toast or English muffin
1 cup heavy cream or sour cream
4 tablespoons brandy (optional)

Heat 32 medium-sized fresh, canned, or frozen mushroom caps in 1/4 cup butter or margarine with 1 tablespoon lemon juice, 1/2 teaspoon salt, few grains of pepper, and 1 tablespoon chopped parsley. For each serving set a round piece of buttered toast or a halved and toasted English muffin on a heatproof baking dish. Pile the mushroom caps neatly in a pyramid on top of the toast. Pour 1 cup heavy cream (sweet or sour) over the mushrooms. Cover with glass bell or custard cup and bake in a moderate oven, 350° F., about 20 minutes. Cream will amalgamate deliciously with the toast and mushrooms.

SERVES 4.

At Serving Time:

If you have classic bells, leave them in place and bring the mushrooms to the table. If you are using custard cups, remove them and dramatize the service by serving your mushrooms flambé: Slightly warm 4 tablespoons brandy over a candle flame. Set alight and pour over mushrooms. The flame lasts only a fraction of a minute but the effect is lovely and the flavor added by the brandy is considerable.

SCALLOPED SWEET POTATOES WITH APPLES

YOU WILL NEED:

2 cups canned sweet potatoes, drained
2 cups canned apple slices, drained
   (retain juice)
1/4 cup dark-brown sugar
1/4 cup butter or margarine
2 teaspoons lemon juice
1/2 teaspoon nutmeg, mace, or allspice
Grated lemon rind

Cut 2 cups canned, drained sweet potatoes into slices about 1/4-inch thick. Arrange in layers in a buttered baking dish along with an equal quantity of canned apple slices, also drained. Sprinkle layers with 1/4 cup dark-brown sugar, 1/4 cup butter or margarine, 2 teaspoons lemon juice, 1/2 teaspoon nutmeg, mace, or allspice. The top layer should be potatoes. Bake in a hot oven, 400° F., about 20 minutes or until thoroughly heated and browned on top. If the casserole seems dry, pour over about 1/2 cup of the juice from the can of apples.

SERVES 6.

At Serving Time:

Decorate the top with thin slivers of lemon rind. This dish is particularly delicious with chicken in any form, ham, or pork.

Sauces for a Gourmet in a Hurry

Top rank in the hierarchy of culinary artists has always been reserved—and most properly—for the *saucier*, the chef who makes the sauces. The perfect sauce is the zenith, the *ne plus ultra* of gastronomic accomplishment and appreciation. Up to now the art of sauce-making has always been long and demanding. Formerly a great deal of time was consumed in the reduction, or boiling down, of liquid necessary for the rich concentration of flavors that is the essence of the fine sauce. More time and skill were consumed in the slow simmering required for a perfect blending of various ingredients.

The requirements of a good sauce are still the same as they have always been—the methods used to accomplish the *saucier*'s aims also remain the same. But in a small and inexpensive can of condensed soup it is possible to find almost the same concentration of flavor, the same blending of ingredients—all done for you!

In addition to the sauces made from various canned condensed soups or from canned beef gravy or canned spaghetti sauce, you will find in this chapter a number of cold sauces with a prepared mayonnaise base. Some of these, such as Ravigote, Vinaigrette, and Gloucester, are particularly valuable for adding an extra note to canned cooked or quick-frozen seafood or to delicatessen cold cuts.

There are times when you will want to use prepared consommés, bouillon, broth, and stock rather than creamed soups or canned gravies. And for these many occasions we have evolved an off-again, on-again technique that makes silken-smooth and shiny sauce every time with never a lump or any suspicion of uncooked-flour flavor.

Still in this realm of saucery, another horizon has been opened through the electric blender. Now it is easy, fast, and sure to achieve in moments even the sauces known for generations as difficult and tricky to make. Hollandaise and its myriad variations, for instance, are all made in a whiz and a whir. Your own mayonnaise takes little more effort than opening a jar.

And because butter—plain, whipped, melted, or seasoned—is probably the most ubiquituous and popular dress-up for everything from biscuits and baked potatoes to pancakes and lobster, we are including here a recipe for blender-churning your own butter, transforming regular into fancy whipped, and making delicate whipped or subtly flavored butter sauces.

SHORTCUT BÉCHAMEL SAUCE

This is one of the classic sauces of the great French cuisine. Formerly, the perfect béchamel sauce required considerable doing and more than a little skill. But now that we have condensed cream of chicken soup, it couldn't be simpler.

YOU WILL NEED:

1 ($10^3/4$-ounce) can condensed cream
   of chicken soup
$1/4$ to $1/2$ cup milk or cream

To a can of condensed cream of chicken soup, add $1/4$ to $1/2$ cup of milk or cream, depending on how thick a sauce you want. Heat and stir, preferably in the top of a double boiler. Strain if you wish, though actually it isn't necessary.

MAKES 2 CUPS.

At Serving Time:

Pass in a separate heated bowl or pour over chicken, fish, or vegetables.

SAUCE SUPREME

Sauce supreme is what makes Chicken Supreme and glamorizes many other foods—such as eggs, fish, and vegetables.

YOU WILL NEED:

1 (10³/₄-ounce) can condensed cream
   of chicken soup
¹/₂ cup light cream
1 or 2 slightly beaten egg yolks or 1
   whole egg
Nutmeg
2 teaspoons lemon juice

To 1 can condensed cream of chicken soup, add ¹/₂ cup light cream. Stir, warm, and strain out bits of chicken and rice. Just before serving stir in 1 or 2 slightly beaten egg yolks or 1 whole egg. Season with a few grains nutmeg and 2 teaspoons lemon juice.

MAKES 2 CUPS.

At Serving Time:

Pour the sauce over and around meat, poultry, or fish. When serving it with vegetables pour it in a wide ribbon over the top of the vegetables and pass a separate bowl of sauce.

SAUCE VELOUTÉ

Forget everything you have read in the old cookbooks! This homemade sauce is made from exactly the same ingredients as the old-fashioned long-simmered type but it takes less than 5 minutes to make. What is even more revolutionary, it does not require more than one pan. It does not call for hot liquid and is absolutely guaranteed not to lump.

YOU WILL NEED:

2 tablespoons butter or margarine
4 tablespoons flour
1 cup chicken, fish, or veal stock
1 cup milk or light cream
Salt, pepper
¼ cup sherry, Madeira, or port

In a small, heavy pan, melt 2 tablespoons butter or margarine. Off heat, stir in 4 level tablespoons flour and smooth together. Return to heat. Cook and stir 2 minutes. If you want a snowy, white sauce, be careful that the butter does not brown. The mixture should not retain any floury taste. Off heat once more, add, all at once, 1 cup stock and 1 cup milk or cream. Bring to boil slowly, once again, stirring always in one direction. Let boil 1 minute. Add salt, pepper, and wine for flavoring, after removing from heat.

MAKES 2¼ CUPS SAUCE.

At Serving Time:

A superlative mask for leftover sliced chicken, turkey, veal loaf, quartered hard-cooked eggs, cauliflower, or mixed cooked vegetables.

CHINESE DUCK SAUCE

Not only with duck but with Chinese egg rolls, barbecued spareribs, roast pork or ham, almost any kind of curry or a rice pilaf, no relish is more delightful than the so-called duck sauce, which can be procured in cans from the Orient and bought in Chinese shops or sometimes in fancy food stores. But what a joy it is to be able to evolve it yourself in just about 15 seconds in your blender and from easy-to-get ingredients!

YOU WILL NEED:

1 cup plum or peach jam or preserves
1 teaspoon Kitchen Bouquet or soy
    sauce
1/4 cup cider vinegar
1/4 teaspoon ground allspice
1 teaspoon dry mustard

Place in the electric blender 1 cup of any kind of plum or peach
jam or preserves. Add 1 teaspoon Kitchen Bouquet or soy sauce
to give the authentically rich brown look. Add 1/4 cup cider
vinegar, 1/4 teaspoon ground allspice, and 1 teaspoon dry
mustard. Cover and blend until very smooth. This will take
about 15 seconds.

MAKES ABOUT 1 1/2 CUPS.

At Serving Time:

Bring to the table in an Oriental-looking bowl or jar, or if you
want to be more Chinese, serve individual dabs in tiny saucers as
in a Chinese restaurant. Usually with Chinese egg roll a dab of
hot mustard is presented at the same time.

ITALIAN SPAGHETTI SAUCE WITH MEAT

*A number of excellent tomato sauces with meat are on the market. But
even if you should have nothing on hand but a can of tomato soup and
1/2 pound hamburger, this sauce can be put together in a very few
minutes.*

YOU WILL NEED:

1 medium onion, chopped
1 clove garlic, crushed
1/2 pound chopped beef
2 tablespoons olive oil, butter or
    margarine, or salad oil

1 (10³/₄ ounce) can condensed tomato
   soup
1 bay leaf

Brown 1 chopped medium-sized onion, 1 crushed clove garlic, and ¹/₂ pound chopped lean beef in 2 tablespoons olive oil, butter or margarine, or salad oil for about 8 minutes, or until the meat has lost its red color. Add 1 can condensed tomato soup, 1 bay leaf, ¹/₄ soup-can water. Simmer 15 minutes to ¹/₂ hour.

MAKES ABOUT 2 CUPS.

At Serving Time:

Remove bay leaf. Taste and add extra salt and pepper if desired. Serve with spaghetti, macaroni, or rice.

MINT SAUCE

Mint sauce is delightful not only with the traditional roast leg of lamb but also with lamb chops. It is good, too, on a salad of Boston lettuce and sliced tomatoes—a boon to calorie counters.

YOU WILL NEED:

1 tablespoon confectioner's sugar
¹/₂ cup vinegar
¹/₄ cup finely chopped fresh or 2
   tablespoons dried mint leaves

Dissolve 1 tablespoon confectioner's sugar in ¹/₂ cup vinegar. If the vinegar is very strong, dilute it with water. Pour over ¹/₄ cup finely chopped mint leaves or about 2 tablespoons dried mint flakes. Let stand about 30 minutes in a warm place.

MAKES ABOUT ¹/₂ CUP.

At Serving Time:

Pass in a small pitcher with lamb. Good on sliced tomatoes, too.

BROWN SAUCE OR GRAVY

Many and varied are the methods for preparing this basic sauce. We will leave to the other cookbooks the chore of preparing gravies from scratch and concentrate on the glamorizing of the canned variety.

YOU WILL NEED:

1 (10-ounce) can beef gravy
1/2 teaspoon Kitchen Bouquet
1 tablespoon red wine or ketchup
Chopped parsley or chives

Canned beef gravy actually needs nothing but heating. However, for a richer color and more interesting flavor, we suggest that you add to a 10-ounce can beef gravy 1/2 teaspoon Kitchen Bouquet, 1 tablespoon or more red wine, or 1 tablespoon tomato ketchup. Heat thoroughly before using.

MAKES ABOUT 2 CUPS.

At Serving Time:

Serve with or over sliced cooked or roast meats. Especially good with leftovers. A sprinkle of chopped parsley or chives is always attractive.

SALMI SAUCE

A hot and savory sauce redolent of sherry or port, this delicious concoction is said to date back to the Middle Ages. It is particularly good with cubed leftover lamb, ham, or pork.

YOU WILL NEED:

1 (10-ounce) can beef gravy
1/4 cup currant jelly
Cayenne
2 tablespoons sherry or port
Parsley or chives (optional)

To 1 (10-ounce) can beef gravy, add ¼ cup currant jelly and a dash of cayenne. Heat and stir until jelly is melted.

MAKES ABOUT 2 CUPS.

At Serving Time:

Add 2 tablespoons sherry or port. A little chopped parsley or chives may be used if desired.

RAVIGOTE SAUCE

Pickled pigs' feet or lambs' tongues in jars are among the less usual ready-to-serve meats. They are surprisingly delicious when served with this herb-flecked sauce.

YOU WILL NEED:

1 cup olive or salad oil
⅓ cup vinegar
Salt and pepper to taste
2 tablespoons capers

1 tablespoon chopped parsley
1 tablespoon chopped onion
1 teaspoon tarragon
1 teaspoon chives

Into a small bowl put 1 cup olive or salad oil, ⅓ cup vinegar, a little salt and pepper, 2 tablespoons capers, 1 tablespoon each finely chopped parsley and onion, 1 teaspoon each tarragon and chives. If you have no fresh tarragon, 1 tablespoon of tarragon vinegar may be used but do not use all tarragon vinegar because the flavor is too strong. Mix thoroughly.

MAKES 1½ CUPS.

At Serving Time:

Pass in a separate bowl or pour around sliced cold cuts such as tongue, meat loaf, etc. If you are serving canned pigs' feet or pickled lambs' tongues, a few tablespoons of liquor from the jar may be stirred into the sauce.

CURRY SAUCE

This is admittedly an Anglicized version of this famous East Indian sauce. You can make it as delicate or as fiery as you wish by increasing the amounts of curry powder.

YOU WILL NEED:

1 (10³/₄-ounce) can condensed cream
   of chicken soup
1 tablespoon curry powder
¹/₄ to ¹/₂ cup evaporated milk or light
   cream
¹/₄ teaspoon ginger or garlic powder
   (optional)
2 tablespoons butter or margarine
   (optional)
1 small apple (optional)
1 small onion, chopped (optional)

To 1 can condensed cream of chicken soup, add 1 flat table-spoon curry powder. Stir in ¹/₄ to ¹/₂ cup evaporated milk or light cream; ¹/₄ teaspoon ginger or garlic powder may be added if desired. For an even better flavor you should lightly brown in 2 tablespoons butter 1 small apple, peeled and diced, and 1 small onion, chopped. Heat everything together and cook for 2 or 3 minutes.

MAKES 1 ¹/₂ TO 2 CUPS.

At Serving Time:

Add to this sauce, quartered or halved hard-cooked eggs, shrimp, crabmeat, or diced cooked chicken. Serve with rice and other curry accompaniments: chutney, salted almonds, India relish, grated coconut, chopped green pepper.

SWEET AND SOUR SAUCE

This versatile sauce, made surprisingly from canned consommé and gingersnaps, does miraculous things for delicatessen meats such as sliced tongue, boiled ham, or sliced roast beef.

YOU WILL NEED:

1 can consomme
1/4 cup cider vinegar
1 small onion, thinly sliced
1/4 cup raisins
1 small lemon, sliced paper-thin
1/4 cup brown sugar
1/2 teaspoon whole allspice
1 bay leaf
Cayenne
6 gingersnaps

Combine 1 can consommé, 1 soup-can water, 1/4 cup cider vinegar. Then add 1 small onion sliced thin, 1/4 cup raisins, 1 small lemon sliced paper-thin, 1/4 cup brown sugar, 1/2 teaspoon whole allspice, 1 bay leaf, and a few grains cayenne pepper. Simmer all together until lemon and onions are tender. Crumble 6 gingersnaps into the sauce. Stir until sauce is smooth and slightly thickened. Do not strain.

MAKES ABOUT 2¹/₂ CUPS.

At Serving Time:

Arrange slices of tongue, ham, or beef in a heatproof serving dish. Pour the sauce over the meat and heat for a minute or so. Garnish with parsley or watercress.

QUICK ROBERT SAUCE

Using canned beef gravy, this piquant and interesting sauce is made in literally a matter of minutes.

YOU WILL NEED:

1 (10-ounce) can beef gravy
1/2 teaspoon bottled gravy-browning
   liquid
1 tablespoon vinegar
1 tablespoon finely chopped shallot or
   onion
1 tablespoon capers
1 tablespoon chopped pickle
Cayenne
6 green olives (optional)
1/2 teaspoon yellow mustard (optional)

To 1 (10-ounce) can beef gravy, add 1/2 teaspoon bottled gravy-browning liquid to darken the color and brighten the flavor. Also add 1 tablespoon each vinegar, finely chopped shallot or onion, capers, chopped pickle, and a few grains cayenne pepper. A half-dozen plain or stuffed green olives, chopped, and 1/2 teaspoon prepared yellow mustard may be added if desired.

SERVES 4 TO 6.

At Serving Time:

Pass sauce separately in a heated bowl or pour over beef, lamb, veal, or pork.

HOLLANDAISE SAUCE

There need never be another curdled hollandaise! With the magic of a blender, a perfect hollandaise equal to that served in the best French restaurants can be made in less than a minute. The recipe is foolproof. All you do is blend hot melted butter into egg yolks and the sauce is ready to serve.

YOU WILL NEED:

1/2 cup (1 stick) butter or margarine
3 egg yolks
2 tablespoons lemon juice

1/4 teaspoon salt
Cayenne

In a small saucepan heat 1/2 cup (1 stick) butter to bubbling, but do not let it brown. Into blender container put 3 egg yolks, 2 tablespoons lemon juice, 1/4 teaspoon salt, and a pinch of cayenne. Cover container and turn motor on high. Immediately remove cover and quickly pour in the hot butter in a steady stream. When all the butter is added, turn off motor. For larger quantity, use 4 egg yolks, 1 cup butter.

MAKES ABOUT 1 CUP.

At Serving Time:

Serve immediately or keep warm (180° F.) by setting the container into a saucepan containing 2 inches hot, not boiling, water. Serve with cooked broccoli, asparagus, cauliflower, or with poached fish or poached eggs.

SOUR CREAM "HOLLANDAISE"

Another ingenious way to approximate hollandaise makes use of commercially soured cream—the kind you buy in cartons.

YOU WILL NEED:

1/2 cup sour cream
2 tablespoons butter or margarine,
    softened
2 tablespoons lemon juice
Cayenne
Salt to taste

Warm 1/2 cup sour cream in the top of a double boiler, but do not allow it to get hot. Stir into it 2 tablespoons softened butter combined with 2 tablespoons lemon juice. Season with a few grains cayenne pepper and a little extra salt, if desired. This sauce may be made ahead of time. It need not be hot, only lukewarm, since it is served over hot vegetables, chicken, fish, or eggs.

MAKES ABOUT 1 CUP, OR 6 TO 8 SERVINGS.

At Serving Time:

Use as a garnish for, or pass separately with, cooked asparagus, broccoli, cauliflower. Can also be used for Eggs Benedictine (see page 39).

SAUCE BÉARNAISE

This classic sauce is actually a hollandaise flavored with tarragon.

YOU WILL NEED:

2 tablespoons white wine
1 tablespoon tarragon vinegar
2 teaspoons chopped fresh or 1
   teaspoon dried tarragon
2 teaspoons chopped shallots or onion
1/4 teaspoon freshly ground black
   pepper
1 cup Hollandaise Sauce (see page 152)

In a skillet combine 2 tablespoons white wine, 1 tablespoon tarragon vinegar, 2 teaspoons chopped fresh or 1 teaspoon dried tarragon, 2 teaspoons chopped shallots or onion, and 1/4 teaspoon freshly ground black pepper. Bring liquid to a boil and cook rapidly until almost all liquid disappears. Pour remaining mixture into hollandaise sauce; cover and blend on high speed for 4 seconds.

MAKES 1 CUP.

At Serving Time:

Serve with broiled steak or chops.

VINAIGRETTE SAUCE

For asparagus, broccoli, cauliflower, green beans, and also for fish, this simplest of sauces may be made from prepared French dressing or from oil and vinegar.

YOU WILL NEED:

1/2 cup French dressing
3 tablespoons India relish
1 teaspoon finely chopped parsley or
    chives (optional)

To 1/2 cup bottled or homemade French dressing add 3 tablespoons chopped India relish; 1 teaspoon finely chopped parsley and/or 1 teaspoon finely chopped chives may be added if desired. Stir well. Heat if you wish, or serve cold.

MAKES ABOUT 1/2 CUP.

At Serving Time:

Stir again just before serving to make sure that the ingredients are well blended. Pass separately or pour over vegetables, fish, or sliced meats such as tongue, ham, or lamb.

SAUCE MAYONNAISE

Mayonnaise and a variety of delectable mayonnaise sauces for seafood or salad greens can be made in your blender in a matter of seconds. This new faster technique makes the recipe foolproof.

YOU WILL NEED:

2 eggs
1/2 teaspoon dry mustard
1/2 teaspoon salt
1/8 teaspoon pepper

1/4 cup vinegar or lemon juice
2 cups salad oil
Tabasco

Place 2 eggs in blender along with 1/2 teaspoon dry mustard, 1/2 teaspoon salt, 1/8 teaspoon pepper, 1/4 cup vinegar or lemon juice, 1/2 cup salad oil, and a couple of drops of Tabasco. Cover container and turn motor on high. Immediately remove cover and quickly add 1 1/2 cups oil in a steady stream. When all the oil is added, turn off motor.

MAKES ABOUT 2¹/₂ CUPS.

At Serving Time:

Pass in a chilled bowl.

MAYONNAISE CHAUD-FROID

The flavor of the chaud-froid is extremely delicate and its goodness depends on the quality of the mayonnaise.

YOU WILL NEED:

1 envelope unflavored gelatin,
  softened in 2 tablespoons cold water
1¹/₂ cups hot water
2 cups mayonnaise

To make a thin, smooth, professional glaze, soften 1 envelope unflavored gelatin in 2 tablespoons cold water. Add 1¹/₂ cups hot water enough to dissolve the gelatin. Stir well until it has cooled to lukewarm. Then mix into it 2 cups mayonnaise.

Coat cooked fish or fowl at once before the mayonnaise has become jellied. Just spread it on thinly, using a spoon as though it were a trowel, and smooth as you go.

MAKES 2 CUPS.

At Serving Time:

Decorate with black olives or truffles or circles of carrot. Be discreet about how much to decorate.

GLOUCESTER SAUCE

This is one of the "cold English sauces," recommended by Escoffier himself, to be served with cold meats. We suggest also that it makes an excellent dressing for egg or fish salads.

YOU WILL NEED:

1 cup mayonnaise made from olive oil
$1/4$ cup sour cream
$1^1/_2$ tablespoons lemon juice
$1/2$ teaspoon Worcestershire sauce
Chopped dill, fennel, parsley, or chives

To 1 cup mayonnaise, add $1/4$ cup sour cream. Stir well and add gradually $1^1/_2$ tablespoons lemon juice and $1/2$ teaspoon Worcestershire sauce.

MAKES 1¼ CUPS.

At Serving Time:

Place in a small bowl in the center of a platter on which you serve sliced cold cuts, or spread over the top of egg or fish salads. In either case, sprinkle the sauce lightly with chopped dill, fennel, parsley, or chives.

TARTARE SAUCE

To many people, fried fish, scallops, or oysters would be unthinkable without tartare sauce. This is a particularly easy and tasty version.

YOU WILL NEED:

$1/2$ cup mayonnaise
$1/2$ cup India relish
$1/2$ tablespoon finely chopped onion or
    parsley (optional)

Stir together $1/2$ cup mayonnaise and $1/2$ cup India relish; $1/2$ tablespoon finely chopped onion or parsley may be added. Chill.

MAKES ABOUT ¾ CUP.

At Serving Time:

It's a pretty thought to serve tartare sauce in lemon or lime shells as a garnish for a platter of fried fish.

SAUCE À LA RITZ

This is somewhat similar to a mayonnaise but with the distinctly Provençal flavor of tomatoes and garlic.

YOU WILL NEED:

1 large egg
1/2 teaspoon dry mustard
1/2 teaspoon salt
2 tablespoons lemon juice
1 cup salad oil
1 tomato, peeled and quartered
1 tablespoon chili sauce
1 clove garlic, crushed
2 tablespoons parsley clusters

In blender container put 1 large egg, 1/2 teaspoon dry mustard, 1/2 teaspoon salt, 2 tablespoons lemon juice, and 1/4 cup salad oil. Cover container and turn motor on high. Immediately remove cover and quickly add 3/4 cup oil in a steady stream. Turn off motor. Add 1 fresh tomato, peeled and quartered; 1 tablespoon chili sauce; 1 clove garlic, crushed; and 2 tablespoons parsley clusters, and stir with rubber spatula to combine. Cover and blend on high speed for 6 seconds.

MAKES ABOUT 1 1/2 CUPS.

At Serving Time:

Serve instead of regular mayonnaise.

AMANDINE SAUCE

With sautéed fish or over such vegetables as asparagus, broccoli, and cauliflower, nothing is better than a sauce of almonds. To save yourself the trouble of blanching, soaking, and shredding the nuts, why not buy a small bag of salted almonds? Or a can of sliced, blanched almonds?

YOU WILL NEED:

1/2 cup butter or margarine
1/4 cup coarsely chopped salted
   almonds
2 or 3 teaspoons lemon juice
Salt and pepper to taste
Chopped parsley or chives (optional)

Use the fat remaining in the pan after frying fish or meat; add enough butter to make about 1/2 cup. Stir until well browned. Add 1/4 cup coarsely chopped salted almonds, 2 or 3 teaspoons lemon juice, and salt and pepper to taste.

At Serving Time:

Pour over or around fried fish, chicken, or cooked asparagus, cauliflower, or broccoli. A sprinkle of chopped parsley or chives may be added if desired.

HOME-CHURNED BUTTER

Sweet whipped unsalted butter—the gourmet's delight—can be yours anytime.

YOU WILL NEED:

1 carton heavy whipping cream (40%
   butter fat)

Break surface of cream in blender and blend. After the cream turns to butter, take out of blender and place in bowl of cold water. This is done to remove the milk from the butter so that it will not sour.

MAKES 1/2 CUP BUTTER.

At Serving Time:

Serve at room temperature.

HOMEMADE WHIPPED BUTTER

For spreading bread with butter to serve as the English do at tea time, for making all sorts of sandwiches, or just to set on the table in an attractive bowl or to serve on pancakes, whipped butter is incomparable.

In certain markets in larger towns and cities whipped butter is always available, but plain stick butter is much easier to come by.

The next recipe will give you directions for transforming heavy cream into whipped butter. This one does it in reverse, by adding a small amount of cream to plain butter. If you prefer, margarine can be substituted for butter in the following recipes.

YOU WILL NEED:

1/2 pound butter
1/2 cup cream

Let a 1/2 pound butter stand at room temperature until it becomes malleable. Break into pieces and place in beater bowl along with 1/2 cup cream. Beat at low speed until all the liquid has been absorbed. Sweet or salted butter may be used.

MAKES 1 1/2 CUPS.

At Serving Time:

Place in an attractive bowl or crock. Serve at "cool-room" temperature. When too cold, whipped butter loses its character.

Variations:

Lingonberry Butter

At the famous Pancake House in Portland, Oregon, they serve along with their incredible Swedish and German pancakes a whipped butter made by beating together equal quantities of whipped butter and lingonberry preserves, which you can get in any fine food shop. The lingonberry is a very small Swedish berry akin to our cranberry. In Germany it is called *Preiselbeeren*. The lingonberries may be added to the softened stick butter and cream all at the same time.

Whipped Honey Butter

Use honey instead of lingonberry preserves, but only 1/2 as much; i.e., 1/4 pound butter, 4 tablespoons cream, 4 tablespoons honey. This makes 1 cup of whipped honey butter. Delicious on pancakes, waffles, French toast, or regular toast.

Salads—Hearty and Otherwise

The salad is the dream of the hurried gourmet, since preparation is reduced to a minimum and the most dramatic effects can be secured with the least possible effort. On one point, however, you must not skimp or hurry, and that is in the careful washing of the greens. Formerly we were told that salad greens should be washed as soon as they came from the garden or market, but now we are assured by the experts that it's best to wash them as you need them. Salting the water is helpful, and in cold weather it is not necessary to freeze your hands—adding a bit of warm water does no harm.

Careful drying with a clean soft towel or paper towel is just about as important as thorough washing, for wet greens mean a watery dressing. Salad greens should be crisp and well chilled.

So much for the mundane requirements of a good salad. The rest is art. Fantasy and imagination play a large part in successful salads, but nowadays it is well to remember that the most effective salads are casual.

TOSSED GREEN SALAD

Combine several different kinds of greens—romaine as well as iceberg lettuce, escarole, chicory, watercress. Whenever possible include the less usual types of greens—dandelion greens in season, corn salad, Boston lettuce, peppergrass, endive, and tender young leaves of spinach.

YOU WILL NEED:

1 clove garlic (optional)
2 cups salad greens
3/4 teaspoon salt
Freshly ground black pepper
4 tablespoons olive oil
1 tablespoon vinegar or lemon juice

Rub a large salad bowl with a cut clove garlic. Place in the bowl about 2 cups well-washed and dried, crisp, chilled salad greens.

SERVES 3 TO 4.

At Serving Time:

Sprinkle greens with 3/4 teaspoon salt and a liberal sprinkling of freshly ground black pepper from the mill. Very slowly add 4 tablespoons olive oil, tossing the greens lightly with fork and spoon until every leaf glistens. Then sprinkle with 1 tablespoon vinegar or lemon juice. Toss again—but not enough to wilt the salad. Taste a leaf and if necessary correct the seasoning. Serve immediately on chilled plates.

Variations:

Tossed Green Salad with Fruit

One of the most delightful fruit salads is nothing more than a tossed green salad to which is added 1/2 to 1 cup well-drained quick-frozen fruit salad or sections of oranges, tangerines, pineapple wedges, or grapefruit sections. Omit garlic. Lemon juice is often preferred to vinegar for fruit salads.

Tossed Green Salad with *Chapon*

Instead of rubbing the salad bowl with garlic, cut the heel off a loaf of French bread or a crusty French roll, rub well with garlic or insert a half clove of garlic into the bread. Toss this bit of bread with the salad to impart a delicate flavor of garlic. Remove the crust of bread—*chapon*—or leave it for those who love it.

Tossed Green Salad with Vegetables

To the classic tossed green salad add ½ to 1 cup well-drained and chilled, cooked or canned vegetables, or raw vegetables, cut into thin slivers or slices.

TOSSED GREEN SALAD AUX FINES HERBES

Sprinkle salad greens with 2 tablespoons finely chopped fresh parsley or chives, or use 1 tablespoon chopped fresh basil, chervil, mint, or tarragon. If you wish, you may use a combination of these various herbs. It is possible to use dried herbs for salad, but they should first be allowed to stand at least 10 minutes in a little of the vinegar or olive oil you are using in your salad. Don't forget that 1 teaspoon of dried herbs is equivalent to 1 tablespoon of fresh herbs.

KING CRAB SALAD MACÉDOINE

An excellent party dish.

YOU WILL NEED:

4 (6-ounce) packages frozen king
    crabmeat
2 (10-ounce) packages frozen peas
2 cups sliced celery
2 cups mayonnaise
2 teaspoons lemon juice
2 teaspoons grated horseradish
½ teaspoon curry powder
2 teaspoons salt
Salad greens

Defrost 4 (6-ounce) packages frozen king crabmeat, then drain.

Cook 2 (10-ounce) packages frozen peas in a small amount of boiling salted water, drain, and chill. Mix 2 cups sliced celery, 2 cups mayonnaise, 2 teaspoons lemon juice, 2 teaspoons grated horseradish, 1/2 teaspoon curry powder, 2 teaspoons salt.

SERVES 12.

At Serving Time:

Toss all ingredients together. Serve on bed of greens.

HOT POTATO SALAD

YOU WILL NEED:

1 large package frozen presliced frying
   potatoes
4 thick slices bacon
1/4 cup chopped onion or 1 tablespoon
   instant onion
1/3 cup malt or cider vinegar
1/4 cup water
2 tablespoons sugar
1 teaspoon dry mustard

Cook 1 package presliced frying potatoes according to package directions. Drain. Cook 4 slices fairly thick bacon until crisp. Remove bacon from pan. Add to the bacon drippings, in the same pan, 1/4 cup finely chopped onion or 1 tablespoon instant onion that has been soaked in a small amount of water. Cook 3 minutes longer. Add 1/3 cup malt or cider vinegar, 1/4 cup water, 2 tablespoons sugar, and 1 teaspoon dry mustard. Mix to a paste with a little water. Bring to a boil and simmer 3 minutes.

SERVES 6.

At Serving Time:

Pour hot bacon mixture over cooked potatoes, serving immediately.

LEAF SPINACH SALAD WITH MYSTERIOUS DRESSING

The secret of this delicious yogurt and chili sauce dressing comes from "a man who got it from a chef who says that it used to be served a generation ago in a famous men's club in Los Angeles."

YOU WILL NEED:

2 packages frozen leaf spinach
2 tablespoons salad oil
2 tablespoons lemon juice
1 cup plain yogurt
1/2 cup chili sauce
1 tablespoon Worcestershire sauce
1 tablespoon prepared mustard
1 hard-cooked egg, sliced

Cook 2 packages frozen leaf spinach just 1 minute—actually just long enough to thaw completely. Drain and mix with 2 table-spoons salad oil and 2 tablespoons lemon juice. Place in the freezer to chill while you make up the dressing: To 1 cup plain yogurt, add 1/2 cup chili sauce, 1 tablespoon Worcestershire sauce, and 1 tablespoon prepared mustard. Blend with a rotary egg beater until smooth.

SERVES 4 TO 6.

At Serving Time:

Pour the dressing over the seasoned spinach, toss lightly, and garnish with a sliced hard-cooked egg.

FEY GERMAN POTATO SALAD

Thawing and heating frozen French fries in water instead of oil makes a salad with a remarkably different look and taste.

YOU WILL NEED:

1 tablespoon salt
1 package frozen French-fried
  potatoes
1/4 teaspoon salt
1/2 teaspoon sugar
1/4 teaspoon dry mustard
1/8 teaspoon pepper
2 tablespoons vinegar
1/2 cup sour cream
1/4 cup diced cucumber (optional)
Chopped parsley or chives

Fill a deep pot with water and 1 tablespoon salt and bring to boil. Place 1 package frozen French-fried potatoes in deep-fry basket (or a strainer) and lower them into boiling water. Cook 5 minutes. Turn potatoes onto absorbent towels to drain and cool.

Meanwhile, make dressing by combining 1/4 teaspoon salt, 1/2 teaspoon sugar, 1/4 teaspoon dry mustard, 1/8 teaspoon pepper, 2 tablespoons vinegar, 1/2 cup sour cream, and 1/4 cup diced cucumber (optional). Cut potatoes into cubes and place in bowl. Stir dressing into potatoes and place in refrigerator to chill.

SERVES 6.

At Serving Time:

Serve with chopped parsley or chives.

NEO-CAESAR'S SALAD

The original Caesar's salad is an invention from California to which tremendous drama is attached, mainly because it is mixed at the table with a raw egg plopped on top of the greens, Don't worry about any raw-egg taste because the lemon juice used in the dressing and the tossing take care of that. This version is called Neo-Caesar because bread sticks have been substituted for the original croutons and because the whole procedure has been considerably simplified.

YOU WILL NEED:

6 cups assorted salad greens
Garlic
1/2 cup grated Parmesan, Cheddar, or
   blue cheese
1 egg
6 tablespoons lemon juice
3 tablespoons olive or salad oil
Salt and freshly ground black pepper
2 teaspoons Worcestershire sauce
   (optional)
1 cup (4 to 6) Italian bread sticks

Break into bits 6 cups crisp chilled salad greens such as lettuce, romaine, escarole, and chicory. Place in a bowl well rubbed with garlic. Scatter over the greens 1/2 cup freshly grated hard cheese such as Parmesan, Cheddar, or blue cheese.

SERVES 4.

At Serving Time:

Start the ceremony by breaking a raw egg on top of the greens. Sprinkle upon the egg and over the greens 6 tablespoons canned or fresh lemon juice (2 average-sized lemons). Toss lightly and add gradually 3 tablespoons olive or salad oil. Season to taste with salt, freshly ground black pepper, and if desired, 2 teaspoons Worcestershire sauce. At the last minute add 1 cup (4 to 6) Italian bread sticks broken into pieces. Serve immediately.

CHICKEN SALAD WITH WHITE GRAPES

YOU WILL NEED:

2 cups canned or cooked, diced
   chicken

3 tablespoons lime or lemon juice
³/₄ cup mayonnaise or salad dressing
¹/₂ cup heavy cream, whipped
Lettuce or escarole
White grapes

Cut 2 cups canned or leftover cooked chicken into pieces—not too small. Sprinkle with 3 tablespoons lime or lemon juice. Make a foamy salad dressing by adding ³/₄ cup prepared mayonnaise or salad dressing to ¹/₂ cup whipped heavy cream. Add ¹/₂ this dressing to chicken. Mix thoroughly. Pack into oiled bowl or 4 custard cups and allow to stand in the refrigerator until thoroughly chilled.

SERVES 4.

At Serving Time:

Unmold on lettuce leaves on chilled individual plates or small platter. Cover salad with remaining dressing as if you were frosting a cake . Garnish with seedless white grapes. Serve with tiny hot cheese biscuits.

BEET ASPIC RING

A nice change from the ever-present tomato aspic.

YOU WILL NEED:

1 package lemon-flavored gelatin
Beet juice
3 tablespoons vinegar

1 tablespoon horseradish
Salt and pepper to taste
Olive oil

Make up a package of lemon-flavored gelatin according to package directions but instead of water, use juice from canned beets, 3 tablespoons vinegar, 1 tablespoon horseradish, and salt and pepper to taste. Chill until firm in small ring mold, which has been lightly oiled with olive oil.

SERVES 4.

At Serving Time:

Unmold. This can be done most effectively by running a knife blade around the edges of the mold. Place a chilled plate over the mold. Turn upside down so that mold is now on top of plate. Shake the mold slightly in order to loosen the gelatin. It is quite all right to unmold salad ½ hour before using, but be sure to put it back into the refrigerator. Garnish with crisp lettuce leaves and fill center of the mold with coleslaw or sliced cucumbers covered with sour cream.

Variation:

Use canned aspics made with pectin.

TWO-BEAN SALAD

This is an interesting combination of green beans and white limas.

YOU WILL NEED:

2 packages frozen French-style string
   beans
1 cup marinade (see below)
2 cans white lima beans
1 pound frankfurters, cut in thin slices
4 medium-sized tomatoes, peeled and
   cubed
Chopped raw pearl onions to taste
Lettuce

Cook 2 packages frozen French-style string beans according to package directions. Stir in ¼ cup marinade and chill. Place 2 cans drained white lima beans in bowl, stir in ¼ cup marinade and chill. Place 1 pound frankfurters cut in thin slices; 4 medium-sized tomatoes, peeled and cubed; and chopped raw pearl onions to taste in third bowl with ¼ cup marinade. Chill all ingredients.

SERVES 4.

At Serving Time:

Line large, low-walled bowl with lettuce leaves and shredded lettuce. Combine beans and other ingredients into one bowl and cover with last ¼ cup of marinade.

MARINADE

Mix ¼ teaspoon black pepper, 1 teaspoon salt, ⅓ cup wine vinegar, ⅔ cup olive oil, ¼ teaspoon mustard, and finely sliced onions (to taste) and shake thoroughly before use.

CRABMEAT AND AVOCADO SALAD WITH GLOUCESTER SAUCE

This is a pretty—and delicious—main dish at lunch or supper.

YOU WILL NEED:

2 avocados
Lemon juice
2 cups canned or quick-frozen
 crabmeat
1 cup Gloucester Sauce (see pages 156-157)
Finely chopped parsley or chives

Cut 2 medium-sized avocados in half crosswise. Scoop out and cut avocado into cubes. Sprinkle with lemon juice to prevent discoloring. Combine with 2 cups canned or cooked quick-frozen crabmeat, which has been carefully picked over and separated into large flakes. Mix lightly with 1 cup Gloucester Sauce. Place mixture into avocado shells. Cover thickly with finely chopped parsley or chives. Serve immediately.

SERVES 4.

At Serving Time:

Pass extra Gloucester Sauce in a small bowl if desired.

CHEF'S SALAD

Practically anything in the way of meat, cheese, and salad greens can go into a chef's salad. It is basically a mixed green salad made hearty—and hence much more acceptable to men—by the addition of solid food, usually cut into julienne strips.

YOU WILL NEED:

4 cups salad greens
1 clove garlic
1 cup sliced boiled ham, salami, or
    bologna
1 cup sliced cooked chicken or tongue
1/4 pound Swiss cheese, slivered
1 hard-cooked egg, sliced
8 anchovies (optional)
Chopped chives or parsley (optional)
1/2 cup French dressing, or 6
    tablespoons olive or salad oil and 2
    tablespoons vinegar
Salt and freshly ground black pepper
    to taste
Prepared mustard

Put about 4 cups of crisp chilled salad greens into a garlic-rubbed bowl. Arrange on top of the greens in small heaps the following ingredients or any desired combination (everything should be in pieces shaped like matchsticks): 1 cup boiled ham, salami, or bologna, 1 cup cooked chicken or tongue, and 1/4 pound slivered Swiss cheese. Slice a hard-cooked egg and use that along with 8 anchovies to decorate the piles. Sprinkle if desired with chopped chives or parsley.

SERVES 4.

At Serving Time:

At the table add 1/2 cup French dressing. Or "dress" at the table in the French manner by slowly pouring on 6 tablespoons olive or salad oil, mix until the greens glisten, sprinkle with 2 tablespoons vinegar, season to taste with salt, freshly ground black pepper, and a bit of mustard if desired. Serve immediately.

COLESLAW

Served in a large, hollow cabbage, coleslaw can make a most dramatic adjunct to the buffet table. In the garden or at the roadside stand, find a large red cabbage, complete with leaves, or a Savoy-type bright-green cabbage, or a common or garden variety cabbage with leaves. Lay it face down in a sinkful of cold water and swish it around to remove the sand. If it seems a little limp, allow it to remain in the water for an hour.

YOU WILL NEED:
Large head of red cabbage, Savoy, or
  garden variety with leaves
Old-fashioned cooked salad dressing
  or equal parts mayonnaise and sour
  cream
Chopped parsley, chives, or dill
Celery or caraway seeds (optional)

To make shell, cut around top of cabbage with a sharp, sturdy knife, leaving a rim about ³/₄-inch thick. Cut the center part into quarters, loosen at the bottom, and remove the quartered cabbage; then cut out the core. Slice each quarter in very thin strips. Place in bowl and mix with special old-fashioned cooked salad dressing or equal parts mayonnaise and sour cream.

SERVES 6 TO 8.

At Serving Time:

Place slaw in the cabbage shell, sprinkle with freshly chopped parsley, chives, or dill; celery or caraway seeds may be used. Since there is some waste involved in making the shell, you should choose a rather large head of cabbage.

Fresh flowers make a charming garnish for a cabbage shell—pink roses, for instance, or pink zinnias tucked in among the purply leaves, or bright yellow or red garden flowers for a green or green-and-white cabbage.

Breads: Yeasty and Otherwise

For breakfast, lunch, or supper—with appetizers, soups, salads, main dishes—as a dessert or a dessert accompaniment, a hot bread adds interest and variety. Often it makes all the difference between a mere snack and a real meal.

In this section we have collected a number of suggestions for transforming bakeshop breads and rolls quickly and easily into hot breads with homemade fragrance and just-baked flavor.

In addition to ideas for fail-proof, speeded-up yeast doughs, there are recipes that show how partially baked goods—brown 'n' serve breads, refrigerated biscuits—may be presented in ways that are essentially new and exciting but that also hark back to the days of long and lavish feasting.

THE GRANT LOAF

Not so long ago I went to England specifically to learn about spirits—not the ethereal but the drinking type. Naturally I sought out the Grants, whose Stand-fast Scotch is one of the "greats." I discovered that the name of Grant is famous also in another field. Doris (Mrs. William) Grant has invented a loaf of unkneaded bread that has swept the British Isles. Mrs. Grant insists that the flour must be stone-ground, the salt should be sea salt, and the sugar should be Barbados muscovado cane, all of which can be found at health-food stores. But regular brown sugar, honey, or molasses can be substituted.

Like many other perfectionists, she also insists upon fresh, compressed yeast rather than dry yeast. Compressed yeast cake does seem to give a better flavor. Still, if it is too difficult to find, a package of dry yeast will do.

YOU WILL NEED:

1 tablespoon salt
3 pounds whole-wheat flour,
   preferably stone-ground
1 (1-ounce) compressed yeast cake
1 tablespoon Barbados muscovado
   sugar or brown sugar, honey, or
   molasses

Mix 1 tablespoon salt with 3 pounds stone-ground whole-wheat flour. In very cold weather, Mrs. Grant suggests that the flour should be warmed slightly, just enough to take the chill off. Mix 1 ounce fresh yeast and 1 tablespoon Barbados muscovado sugar, brown sugar, honey, or molasses in a small bowl with ½ cup lukewarm water—blood heat is the English term; i.e., 98° F. Leave for 10 minutes or until it becomes frothy. Pour the yeasty liquid into the flour, adding 3½ cups lukewarm water. Beat 2 minutes at low speed. Divide the dough into 3 quart-size bread tins that have been warmed or greased. Or you may use 6 pint-size bread tins to make small loaves. Place the tins in a warm place, about 80° F. Cover with a cloth and leave for about 20 minutes to rise about ⅓ or until dough is within an inch of top of the pan. Bake in a moderately hot oven, 400° F., for about 35 to 40 minutes.

MAKES 3 LARGE OR 6 SMALL LOAVES.

At Serving Time:

Serve this bread warm from the oven with whipped butter. There is no greater delight. To keep the bread in the freezer, it is best to slice and place in plastic bags. In this way the whole loaf need not be defrosted at once. Frozen slices may be popped immediately into the toaster or they may be thawed quickly at room temperature.

HOMEMADE BREAD FROM A MIX

If you want to build up your courage to attempt baking bread, it's a very wise idea to start with a hot-roll mix. You will find in the package all the necessary directions, making failure next to impossible. We have discovered a new (but actually very old) way to give the loaves a highly professional glaze.

YOU WILL NEED:

1 package hot-roll mix
  water or milk
1 egg white, slightly beaten
Melted butter or margarine

Follow directions on the hot-roll mix package. When dough is well risen, punch it down. Turn it out on a floured board and work the dough by folding and turning, rolling and kneading. Unlike pastry, yeast dough takes kindly to handling. According to the directions on some packages, hot-roll mixes do not require kneading, but you will get a closer-textured, finer-grained loaf if you do knead 3 to 5 minutes. After you have shaped the loaves and placed them in greased bread pans (we like to make 2 small loaves from a package of mix rather than 1 large one), brush lightly with melted butter or margarine. Cover with a paper towel. Set in a warm place not above 95° F, 45 to 55 minutes.

If you like a soft and tender crust, brush the tops of the loaves with melted butter 10 minutes before the baking is complete. For a crusty bread, brush the loaves with slightly beaten egg white instead of butter.

MAKES 1 LARGE OR 2 SMALL LOAVES.

EGG-YOLK GLAZE FOR BREADS

YOU WILL NEED:

1 egg yolk
2 tablespoons cold water

Mix with fork 1 egg yolk and 2 tablespoons cold water. Brush over breads just before baking for shiny golden-brown finish.

EGG-WHITE GLAZE

YOU WILL NEED:

1 egg white
2 tablespoons water

Mix one unbeaten egg white and 2 tablespoons water. Brush over breads just before baking for shiny, light finish.

BACON BREAD BAKED IN A CASSEROLE

This amount of batter may be baked in 2 small, well-buttered or well-oiled casseroles holding about 1½ pints each, or in 4 onion-soup ramekins, which hold about 1 cupful each.

YOU WILL NEED:

1 cup hot milk
2½ teaspoons salt
3 tablespoons brown sugar
2 tablespoons bacon drippings
1 egg
2 packages yeast
3½ cups all-purpose flour, sifted
1 cup whole-wheat flour, sifted
⅓ teaspoon ground coriander seeds
2 slices cooked bacon, crumbled
White pepper

Blend in electric blender 1 cup hot milk with 2½ teaspoons salt, 2 tablespoons brown sugar, 2 tablespoons bacon drippings, and 1 egg. Cool to lukewarm.

Meanwhile, measure into a warm mixing bowl 1 cup lukewarm water; add 1 tablespoon brown sugar. Crumble 2 cakes or packages of yeast into the warm water. Stir gently. Allow to stand about 5 minutes, until it looks bubbly. Then add the milk-and-egg mixture from the blender.

Now add 3½ cups sifted all-purpose flour, 1 cup sifted whole-wheat flour, ⅓ teaspoon ground coriander seeds. Beat with electric beater 3 minutes. Cover. Allow to rise in a warm place 82° to 85° F. until twice its size. This will take about 40 minutes. Stir in 2 slices bacon that have been cooked crisp and crumbled. Sprinkle lightly with white pepper. Beat with electric beater 2 minutes longer.

Bake in well-buttered casseroles or baking dishes in an oven preheated to 400° F., about 40 minutes.

At Serving Time:

Turn out of casseroles or serve in baking dishes. This bread is best when slightly warm. It may be sliced in the usual way or in very small pie-shaped wedges. Especially good with sweet butter and whipped cream cheese.

POPOVERS

Even without a mix, popovers are not at all difficult to make and they're so rewarding—if they pop! This recipe is considerably "speeded up"—it eliminates the sifting of flour, the melting of shortening, and it adds, for those who want further insurance, a bit of baking powder.

YOU WILL NEED:

2 eggs, well beaten
1 cup milk
1 tablespoon salad oil
⅞ cup all-purpose flour
¼ teaspoon salt
¼ teaspoon baking powder

Beat 2 eggs until light. Add 1 cup milk and 1 tablespoon salad oil (not olive oil). Beat together with an electric beater. Add ⅞ cup all-purpose flour. Sifting is not necessary but if you wish to sift the flour, then use 1 cup flour measured after sifting. The reason for the difference is quite obvious—sifting aerates flour, makes it less bulky. With the flour add ¼ teaspoon salt and ¼ teaspoon baking powder. Beat until smooth. The mixture should be heavy as whipping cream. If too thick, add a little more milk. Heavy iron muffin pans are generally used for popovers but they are not necessary. You may use aluminum pans if you wish, or ovenproof custard cups. Grease bottom and sides thoroughly. Fill ½ full with mixture. Have the oven preheated to at least 500° F. When the popovers have popped, in about 15 minutes, turn oven down to 400° F. and continue baking 10 to 15 minutes longer or until done. The crust should sound crackly-crisp when tapped with your fingernail, the inside staying pleasantly moist—almost doughy but not wet. To be really sure you must break one open.

MAKES 8.

At Serving Time:

Serve hot with plenty of butter, jam, honey, or preserves with a luncheon salad or a hearty supper soup.

Note: Here are a few pointers on popovers. If you want popovers to "hold over," bake at 500° F. for 15 minutes and then turn oven to 250° F. until done.

How do you know when popovers are "done"? They will have popped way above the pan. They should be crisp, brown, and glossy on the outside and soft but not soggy on the inside. The toothpick is still a good tester. If it comes out dry the popover is cooked enough. If you like dry centers, punch a little hole in the side about 5 minutes before they are ready to come out of the oven. This will let out the steam, making crisp popovers that are excellent to serve along with creamed dishes or with salad and cheese instead of break sticks. Popovers make fine "cases," much easier and just as pretty as patty shells.

Popovers take kindly to freezing, too. No need to thaw; just place frozen into the oven.

ONION ROLLS

YOU WILL NEED:

1/2 cup salad oil
1 small chopped onion
1 package brown 'n' serve rolls
1 very thinly sliced onion
Sesame seeds

Blend 1/2 cup salad oil with 1 small chopped onion and pour into a cup. Now dip the top of each brown 'n' serve roll into the salad-oil mixture and place a thin, thin slice of onion on top. Also sprinkle the top of the rolls with sesame seeds. Bake 6 to 8 minutes at 450° F., 8 to 10 minutes at 425° F., or 10 to 12 minutes at 400°F.

SERVES 4.

At Serving Time:

Serve piping hot with soup, salad, or cheese.

SKILLET SPOON BREAD

Delicious with ham or fried chicken!

YOU WILL NEED:

1/3 cup cornmeal
1/2 teaspoon baking soda
1/2 teaspoon salt
3 eggs
1 cup milk
1 cup buttermilk
1/4 cup butter or margarine

Sift 1/3 cup cornmeal with 1/2 teaspoon baking soda; add 1/2 teaspoon salt. Put 3 eggs into blender with 1 cup milk and 1 cup buttermilk. Combine egg-and-milk mixture with cornmeal mixture and stir. Don't blend. Stir just enough to mix.

Preheat electric skillet with cover on to 460° F. Add ¼ cup butter or margarine and when melted, pour in batter and cook with skillet covered for 25 to 30 minutes, or until brown and puffy.

At Serving Time:

Serve immediately from skillet or it will flatten. Add a dab of butter to each serving if you like.

BRIOCHES FROM A HOT-ROLL MIX

This recipe cuts out half a dozen operations, rises in a third the time, makes a brioche as French as Paris.

YOU WILL NEED:

1 package hot-roll mix
4 egg yolks, beaten
⅛ cup sugar
1 teaspoon grated lemon rind or ¼
    teaspoon powdered cardamom
2 tablespoons butter

Place in a large bowl 1 envelope yeast from 1 package hot-roll mix and dissolve in ¼ cup very warm water; add ⅓ package of the dry mix along with 3 slightly beaten egg yolks, ⅛ cup sugar, 1 teaspoon grated lemon rind or ¼ teaspoon powdered carda- mom. Beat the mixture 3 minutes at high speed with an electric beater. Add the rest of the package of dry mix and mix well. Turn into lightly buttered bowl, cover with a damp towel, and let stand in a warm place until double in bulk. Now chill or not, as you please, 3 hours or overnight. Let rise again until double in bulk.

Now divide dough and reserve ¼ for the traditional little caps to go on top of the brioches. Butter your hands generously and form 12 balls the size of golf balls; form the rest into 12 balls the size of marbles. Grease 12 iron gem pans or fluted brioche molds with butter. Place a large ball in each pan and top with a small ball. Allow to rise again until double in size. Brush with butter- and-egg glaze: 2 tablespoons melted and cooled butter mixed with 1 well-beaten egg yolk. Brioches are baked in an oven slightly less hot than for ordinary rolls, 375° F., for about 20 minutes. Turn out and cool on racks.

MAKES 12.

At Serving Time:

The French never serve brioches warm but we do. They are excellent split crosswise, toasted under the broiler and buttered, or buttered first and then toasted.

QUICK SALLY LUNNS

Who Sally was—where she lived—or how her name happened to be given to this popular Southern tea bread, we have never discovered. Sally appears in many guises in different regions of the country. Risen Sally Lunn is made from a yeast dough but Quick Sally is made with baking powder.

YOU WILL NEED:

2 cups biscuit mix
³/₄ cup milk
3 eggs, well beaten
¹/₄ cup sugar
2 tablespoons butter or margarine

To 2 cups biscuit mix add ³/₄ cup milk, 3 well beaten eggs, ¹/₄ cup sugar, and 2 tablespoons melted butter or margarine. Pour batter into well-greased muffin tins and bake in a hot oven, 400° F., about 15 minutes.

MAKES 12.

At Serving Time:

The old recipes say, "Run with Sally Lunn to the table," for this tea bread must be served so hot that the butter melts into the feathery bread instantly.

Variation:

Angel Sally

Sally Lunn is often baked in an angel-cake pan or a ring mold. The pans should be well greased with butter and the cake baked at 350° F. about 40 minutes.

CINNAMON TOAST LOGS

The vogue for ready-sliced bread has made certain old-fashioned specialties difficult to prepare. Lacking whole bread, these cinnamon logs may be made even with sliced bread, stacked.

YOU WILL NEED:

3 slices bread
Butter or margarine
1 teaspoon cinnamon
3 tablespoons sugar

Butter 3 thin slices of bread. Lay one on top of the other. Remove crust and cut into 3 strips. Brush with melted butter or margarine, roll in a mixture of cinnamon and sugar, using 1 teaspoon cinnamon to 3 tablespoons sugar. Place in a moderate oven until sugar has melted.

SERVES 2.

At Serving Time:

Bring directly from oven to table and serve with tea.

Variation:

Brown Sugar Logs

Use light-brown or old-fashioned dark-brown sugar instead of white.

BOSTON BROWN BREAD

Boston brown bread is now available in cans. Canned brown bread, however, should always be served steamy hot, unless of course it is sliced thin for sandwiches. On most cans of brown bread you will find directions telling you to immerse the can in hot water. This method of heating takes a long time, and what is more important, the hot can is difficult to handle. The method suggested here is much simpler.

YOU WILL NEED:

1 can Boston brown bread

Open a can of brown bread at both ends and push the bread out of the can. Place in the top of a double boiler. Cover and heat over boiling water.

MAKES 10 SLICES.

At Serving Time:

Bring to the table in one piece and slice about ½-inch thick; or slice in the kitchen and serve in a bowl or basket lined with a napkin, with Boston baked beans, of course, coleslaw, and apple pie for dessert.

Grand Cakes Made Easy

Mixes make child's play of baking. But one thing is certain: You must follow the directions on the package to the letter. Then, and only then, will you have perfect cakes, pies, cookies, and cupcakes—with a minimum of time, effort, and expense. Curiously enough, the novice often has better luck with mixes than the experienced baker, probably because she is less likely to improve on them or use older and unsuitable methods.

Here are a few warnings and suggestions that will make baking with mixes easier, faster, surer—and more fun.

Do not sift any kind of mix. It is not necessary, for all ingredients have already been thoroughly combined in the manufacturing.

Do not undermix or overmix. If you have a hand beater, count your strokes. If you use an electric mixer, watch the second hand of your clock or use an egg timer.

Unless you are very sure of yourself and have had a great deal of experience, not only in baking but in baking with mixes, it is wisest not to improvise too much on the basic ingredients: Do not add eggs unless your particular cake mix calls for them; do not use water instead of milk; do not vary the amounts of liquid. There are, however, a number of flavoring and glamorizing tricks that you can safely use. One to 3 teaspoons grated orange rind may be added. Buttermilk may be substituted for sweet milk in devil's-food or chocolate cake mix. One-fourth to $1/2$ teaspoon of extract (orange, lemon, almond, or peppermint) may be added to white or yellow cake. For pistachio flavor use half-and-half vanilla and almond extracts. When spices are added, it is best not to use more than a teaspoon in all. Chopped nuts and/or chopped fruits are good in gingerbread, devil's-food, chocolate, or spice cake mix, but be careful about adding too much to a white cake batter or they will sink to the bottom, because this batter is usually thinner.

Although there is some disagreement even among the experts about the necessity of preheating the oven, you are always on the safe side if you do light the oven about 10 minutes beforehand. Opening the oven door lowers the oven temperature, so do this as little as possible. Do not overbake cakes, cookies, or pastries made from mixes. For a perfect cake, leave it in the oven the minimum time suggested on the package or maybe a few minutes less. If the cake shows just a sign of pulling away from the sides of the pan, it is done. Or place your finger lightly on the cake. If it makes no depression, the cake is done. Or insert a wire cake tester or a clean broom straw. If it comes out clean, the cake is done.

What you do to your cake after you take it from the oven is most important. Set the cake—pan and all—on a wire rack to cool for 5 to 10 minutes. The wire rack allows the air to get under the cake as well as around it. Loosen cake around edges. If a topping is to be baked on, place topping on hot cake. For a boiled or 4-minute frosting, cool cake about 30 minutes before frosting. Buttery frostings should be put on the cake when it is thoroughly cool so that the heat of the cake will not melt the frosting.

Cake Mixes Prepared in the Blender

Some cake mixes but not all can be done in the blender. Best for blender mixing are close-textured cakes, like gingerbread, spice cake, pound cake, and fudge cake mixes.

If eggs are required, put the eggs and half the liquid in the blender. Add the contents of the package of cake mix, then the remaining liquid. Cover and turn on the blender. Run 5 seconds, stop the blender, and stir down the cake batter with a rubber spatula. Now blend 15 seconds longer. Stir down again if necessary.

CHERRY UPSIDE-DOWN CAKE

YOU WILL NEED:

1 no. 2 can pitted red sour cherries
1/4 cup butter or margarine, melted
1/2 cup brown sugar
1 package white cake mix
Almond extract (optional)

Drain syrup from a no. 2 can pitted red sour cherries and save for sauce. Melt 1/4 cup butter or margarine in a heavy frying pan or cake pan and add 1/2 cup brown sugar. Place cherries in the pan close together. Pour on batter made according to directions from a package of white cake mix. Bake at 350° F. about 25 minutes. Cool cake 5 minutes. Invert the pan on a plate and let stand 1 minute before removing pan.

At Serving Time:

At the table, cut into squares and pass separately a sauce made by boiling the syrup down to 1/2 the original quantity. A bit of almond extract may be added to the syrup if desired.

Variations:

Pineapple, Apricot, Peach, or Loganberry Upside-Down Cake

Any of the above fruits, either canned or quick-frozen, may be used instead of cherries. They should be well drained. Pecans may be placed on top of the butter-sugar mixture before the fruit is added.

APPLESAUCE CAKE

Spice cake mix and canned applesauce make a quick, modern version of this wonderful old-fashioned cake, which can also be served warm as a pudding.

YOU WILL NEED:

1 package spice cake mix
1/2 teaspoon baking soda
1/4 teaspoon powdered cloves
1 cup unsweetened applesauce
1 cup raisins and/or chopped nuts
Butter
Flour
Ready-whipped cream or sweetened
   sour cream

Make up a package of spice cake mix according to the package recipe. Add 1/2 teaspoon baking soda, 1/4 teaspoon powdered cloves, 1 cup unsweetened applesauce, 1 cup raisins and/or chopped nuts. Bake in 2 buttered and floured loaf pans. Baking time is slightly longer than cake without applesauce—about 40 minutes in a moderate oven, 350° F., or until done.

At Serving Time:

Cut into slices about 1/2-inch thick. Serve cold, or if desired, cut in squares and serve warm with ready-whipped cream or slightly sweetened sour cream.

BAKED ALASKAS—UNBAKED

This recipe dispenses with all that busy-ness, fol-de-rol of covering a board with brown paper, putting ice cream into the oven, worrisome timing, and worst of all—messy serving.

YOU WILL NEED:

6 cupcake halves or 1/2-inch slices
   sponge cake
6 slices solidly frozen ice cream
3 egg whites
6 tablespoons superfine sugar
Halved eggshells

¹/₄ teaspoon salt, cream of tartar, or
   lemon juice
1 cup cognac, bourbon, or rum

Top six cupcake halves or ¹/₂-inch slices of sponge cake with
solidly frozen ice cream portions. Cover cream completely with
meringue made by beating 3 egg whites until frothy; add ¹/₄
teaspoon salt, cream of tartar, or lemon juice; gradually add 6
tablespoons superfine sugar; keep beating until peaks stand stiff.
Into the top of each peak press a halved eggshell. Warm to body
temperature 1 cup spirits—pour 1 tablespoonful into each
eggshell, set the rest ablaze with a wooden taper or kitchen
match, and pour over the desserts. The flames will set the spirits
in the eggshell afire and the meringue will be set and gilded then
and there.

SERVES 6.

CHOCOLATE PRALINE CAKE

YOU WILL NEED:

1 package chocolate cake mix
¹/₃ cup butter or margarine, melted
¹/₂ cup dark-brown sugar
¹/₄ cup light cream
Dash salt
¹/₂ teaspoon vanilla extract
1 cup shredded coconut

Bake a chocolate cake from a mix in a square or loaf pan. While
the cake is still hot, spread over the top the following mixture: ¹/₃
cup melted butter or margarine, ¹/₂ cup dark-brown sugar, ¹/₄
cup light cream, a dash salt, ¹/₂ teaspoon vanilla extract, 1 cup
shredded coconut. Place under broiler about 5 minutes or until
golden brown and bubbly—or bake in a moderate oven, 350° F.,
about 10 minutes.

At Serving Time:

Cake may be served warm in squares directly from the baking pan, or cold, taken from the pan and served in slices with vanilla ice cream on the side.

BLACK FOREST CAKE

YOU WILL NEED:

1 package chocolate or devil's-food
  cake mix
2 cups sweetened whipped cream or
  whipped topping, or 1 cup heavy
  cream, whipped and sweetened with
  1 tablespoon superfine sugar
2 tablespoons kirsch or white rum
1 envelope unflavored gelatin
1 package frozen black or red cherries
Grated chocolate

Bake in 3 layers a package of chocolate or devil's-food cake mix prepared according to directions. While cake is cooling, combine 2 cups sweetened whipped cream with 2 tablespoons kirsch or white rum and 1 envelope unflavored gelatin that has been soaked in a little cold water. Fold into the cream 1 package frozen black or red cherries, thawed and drained. Cover 2 layers of the cake with this mixture and spread the rest over the entire cake, top and sides. Sprinkle generously with grated chocolate.

At Serving Time:

Place on a cake plate and decorate with nut meats.

CAROLINA TRIFLE

There is no set recipe for this famous English dish. Much depends on the resources of the household at the moment.

YOU WILL NEED:

10 ladyfingers or 10 slices sponge cake
Jam
Sherry, Madeira, or port
3 to 4 tablespoons canned shredded
    almonds
1 tablespoon grated lemon (optional)
1 package custard or vanilla-pudding
    mix
1 cup whipped cream
1 egg white
1/4 teaspoon cinnamon
Candied cherries, preserved
    kumquats, or jelly

Split 10 ladyfingers or use thin, small slices of sponge cake. Spread with jam and arrange in the bottom of a glass bowl. Sprinkle with sherry (Madeira or port may be used). Then add 3 or 4 tablespoons canned shredded almonds and 1 tablespoon grated lemon peel if desired. Over all pour custard made according to package directions from custard-flavored mix or vanilla-pudding mix. Let stand in the refrigerator several hours, or better still, overnight.

SERVES 8 TO 10.

At Serving Time:

Garnish with 1 cup sweetened whipped cream or ready-whipped cream to which has been added 1 stiffly beaten egg white and 1/4 teaspoon cinnamon. Garnish with candied cherries, drained preserved kumquats, or bits of bright jelly or preserves.

INSTANT CHEESE CAKE

Made in the blender with chopped ice, using an amazing new technique, it really is instant. And delicious!

YOU WILL NEED:

2 envelopes unflavored gelatin
Juice of ¹/₂ lemon and thin strip lemon
   peel
¹/₂ cup hot milk
¹/₄ cup sugar
2 egg yolks
8 ounces cream cheese
1 cup crushed ice
¹/₂ cup heavy cream
Zwieback crumbs

Put 2 envelopes gelatin, juice of ¹/₂ lemon, and a thin strip lemon peel into the blender. Add ¹/₂ cup hot milk, cover, and blend on high speed for 40 seconds. Add ¹/₄ cup sugar, 2 egg yolks, and 8 ounces cream cheese; cover and blend on high speed for 10 seconds. Remove cover; add 1 heaping cup crushed ice and ¹/₂ cup heavy cream and continue to blend for 15 seconds. Immediately pour into a 4-cup spring-form pan and sprinkle with zwieback crumbs.
SERVES 6.

At Serving Time:

Serve as is (which is wonderful) or top with sour cream and pieces of fruit or the following glaze:

FRUIT GLAZE FOR CHEESE CAKE, FLANS, FRUIT TARTS

YOU WILL NEED:

1 package raspberry-, cherry-, or
   strawberry-flavored gelatin

1 cup hot water
2 tablespoons currant jelly
1 pint fresh strawberries, whole or
   halved (optional)

Dissolve 1 package raspberry-, cherry-, or strawberry-flavored gelatin in 1 cup hot water. Add 2 tablespoons currant jelly. Swift-chill in freezer 10 minutes or until thick as unbeaten egg whites. Spoon on top of cheese cake. If you like, put 1 pint whole or halved fresh strawberries or other berries on chilled glaze. Chill in refrigerator.

LADY BALTIMORE CAKE

One of the great glories of the table in Maryland and other parts of the South has been the Lady Baltimore cake. A facsimile of this cake can be made from a package of white cake mix and Fluffy Uncooked Frosting (see page 196). Since Lady Baltimore has always been a queenly cake in size as well as delicacy, we suggest using 2 packages of white cake mix.

YOU WILL NEED:

2 packages white cake mix
1/2 teaspoon almond extract or 1
   teaspoon rose flavoring
6 cups Fluffy Uncooked Frosting
1/2 cup chopped pecans
3 dried figs, cut in thin strips
1/2 cup seeded raisins
1/2 teaspoon almond extract

Make up 2 packages white cake mix according to directions. Add 1/2 teaspoon almond extract or 1 teaspoon rose flavoring. Bake in 3 (8-inch) round layer pans in a moderate oven, 375° F., 25 to 30 minutes or until done. Put together with filling and top with frosting as follows:

LADY BALTIMORE FROSTING AND FILLING
Double recipe for Fluffy Uncooked Frosting. Save ¹/₂ the frosting for the top and sides of the cake and to the rest add ¹/₂ cup chopped pecans, 3 dried figs cut into thin strips, ¹/₂ cup seeded raisins cut up, and ¹/₂ teaspoon almond extract.

At Serving Time:

This is a large cake that deserves your prettiest plate or platter and garland of fresh blossoms and green leaves.

MIRACLE FRUIT CAKE

YOU WILL NEED:

1 package spice cake mix	³/₄ cup seedless raisins
¹/₂ teaspoon baking soda	1 cup ready-to-use diced candied
1 teaspoon sherry, rum or	fruits and peels
brandy (optional)	1 egg white, slightly beaten
1 cup sliced pitted dates	Chopped nut meats (optional)

Make up a package of spice cake mix according to package directions, adding ¹/₂ teaspoon baking soda. If desired, up to 1 teaspoon sherry, rum, or brandy may be substituted for an equal quantity of liquid. Combine 1 cup sliced pitted dates with ³/₄ cup seedless raisins and 1 cup ready-to-use diced candied fruits and peels.

Line a pan (19 inches round or square) with greased heavy waxed paper. Put in a layer of batter. Sprinkle with a layer of fruit, then add a layer of batter, alternating fruit and batter until dish is ³/₄ full. The last layer should be batter. Bake in a slow oven, 375° F., about 1 hour or until done. Decorate as follows: 15 minutes before cake is done, brush with 1 slightly beaten egg white; quickly arrange on the cake in a pattern bits of candied fruit, maraschino cherries, and/or chopped nuts. Return to oven. Finish baking.

At Serving Time:

A fruit cake may be brought to the table and served as well as stored in its own casserole. For a gala appearance, pin a napkin around the casserole and decorate with a spray of leaves. To serve fruit cake flambé, slightly warm ¼ cup brandy or rum, set ablaze, and pour over fruit cake. If possible, serve a little flame on each slice. If you store your fruit cake, pour a little brandy over it from time to time to keep it moist. Keep tightly covered in a cool place.

ELECTION CAKE

According to the Browns, learned commentators on culinary matters, the Connecticut Election Cake has always been dedicated to the feasting of both winners and losers. The recipe for this cake was invariably found "sandwiched between household accounts and directions for cough cures in old farm wives' notebooks." The cake is found under various names and with many different ingredients. Sometimes the recipe "was recognizable only by the fact that it was raised with yeast and had fruit in it." Here is an unorthodox version, prepared from a package of hot-roll mix.

YOU WILL NEED:

1 package hot-roll mix
½ cup brandy or rum
Juice of 1 lemon
1 teaspoon grated lemon rind
1 teaspoon cinnamon
½ teaspoon ground nutmeg or mace
1 cup seedless raisins
1 package white frosting mix

Make up a package of hot-roll mix according to package recipe for coffee cake. But for ½ cup of the liquid substitute ½ cup brandy or rum. Add to batter 1 teaspoon lemon juice, 1 teaspoon grated lemon rind, 1 teaspoon cinnamon, and ½ teaspoon nutmeg or mace. When dough has risen to double its bulk, punch it down and add 1 cup seedless raisins. Bake in greased bread pans according to package directions. When cold, cover with frosting made from a mix.

At Serving Time:

Slice as you would bread and serve with coffee. In the old days this cake always ended the veal dinner, which was as essential to Election Day as turkey and pie to Thanksgiving.

FLUFFY UNCOOKED FROSTING

This frosting has the look and flavor of real old-fashioned boiled frosting but no cooking is involved—only a few minutes of beating.

YOU WILL NEED:

1 egg white
³/₄ cup sugar
¹/₄ teaspoon cream of tartar
1 teaspoon vanilla

Combine 1 unbeaten egg white with ³/₄ cup sugar, ¹/₄ teaspoon cream of tartar, and 1 teaspoon vanilla in a small deep bowl and mix well. Add ¹/₄ cup boiling water and beat with a rotary egg beater or at the high speed of an electric mixer until the frosting will stand in stiff little peaks. This should take about 4 minutes. A cake with this frosting should be kept uncovered at room temperature. Don't put it in the refrigerator.

MAKES 3 CUPS, ENOUGH TO COVER TOP AND SIDES OF 2 (8-INCH) LAYERS.

Variations:

Pink Peppermint Frosting

Use above recipe, substituting for the vanilla ¹/₄ teaspoon peppermint extract. Add a few drops of red pure-food coloring to tint delicately. Especially delicious on devil's-food cake.

Pistachio Frosting

Use above recipe and decrease vanilla to ¹/₂ teaspoon. Add ¹/₄ teaspoon almond extract. If desired, tint a delicate green with pure-food coloring and garnish with pistachio nuts.

Orange Frosting

Use above recipe but omit vanilla and substitute for the boiling water 1/4 cup heated canned orange juice.

QUICK FUDGE FROSTING

Several frosting mixes are on the market. To most of these nothing but water and butter need be added. Variations in flavor may be achieved by substituting, for part of the water, a little rum, sherry, brandy, or orange juice. Sweetened condensed milk makes an excellent quick fudge frosting.

YOU WILL NEED:

2 squares unsweetened cooking
   chocolate
1 can sweetened condensed milk
1 teaspoon vanilla and a few grains salt
   or 1/2 teaspoon vanilla and 1/2
   teaspoon almond extract

Put 2 squares unsweetened cooking chocolate into the top of a double boiler along with 1 can sweetened condensed milk. Stir until melted. Add 1 teaspoon vanilla and a few grains of salt or 1/2 teaspoon vanilla and 1/2 teaspoon almond extract. Then, little by little, add about a tablespoon of hot water, just enough to make the frosting thin enough to spread.

Be sure that cake or cupcakes are cool. Brush off loose crumbs. To frost a layer cake, place a little frosting on the bottom layer, spreading it almost to the edge. Set second layer on top, centering it evenly. Then smooth the frosting on outside of cake in sweeping strokes over top edge and down sides. Pile remaining frosting on top, spreading lightly to edges. If you have any difficulty, dip your knife into warm water.

FABULOUS NO-FUSS DESSERTS

To let a meal trail off without a dessert is like staging a play with no finale. Even a simple menu takes on a lavish air when you bring on a dessert of distinction.

It need not be extravagant nor particularly time-consuming. But it should be, in one way or another, a conversation piece.

Even at an impromptu meal you can whip up a soufflé at the last minute just before you sit down to eat. In spite of their temperamental reputation, soufflés can be baked at any temperature from 325° to 450°. So you may time them to suit your own pace.

Here we have collected a galaxy of tried-and-true favorites ... sure and simple soufflés, puddings, pies, custards, crêpes, tarts— even macaroons and bourbon balls.

DINNER TABLE SOUFFLÉ

Because it requires no basic sauce and no previous preparation, this soufflé is ideal to prepare right at the dinner table a few minutes before the guests sit down. Or if you want a longer time to eat, you can prepare the soufflé after the meal has started. Practically any type of liqueur or spirit can be used. Generally, this soufflé is served very soft in the center, and so it is cooked in the French fashion at a fairly high temperature for just about 20 minutes.

Because it contains no thickening, this soufflé is extremely delicate and except in the hands of the most experienced cook it might prove troublesome if you tried to cook it in the kitchen and bring it to the table in the usual way. I bake the soufflé in the rotisserie oven right at the table. Great drama for the guests to watch! If the bell rings before you are ready for your dessert, simply turn the oven down to 300° F. Don't touch; don't peek.

YOU WILL NEED:

5 eggs, separated
1/4 cup superfine sugar
2 tablespoons coffee-flavored cordial
   and 2 teaspoons instant coffee, (rum,
   cognac, or orange juice may be
   substituted for the cordial and
   coffee)

Into the glass container of the blender place 4 egg yolks, 1/4 cup superfine sugar, 2 tablespoons coffee-flavored cordial, and 2 teaspoons instant coffee. Or you may substitute rum, cognac, or orange juice for the cordial and instant coffee. Blend about 20 seconds or until the mixture is thick and pale.

Preheat the oven to 400° F.

Place 5 egg whites in a straight-sided 1 1/2-quart baking dish. (It is the rule in France to use 1 more white than yolk.) Beat the whites until they are stiff but not dry. Pour the egg-yolk mixture onto the whites and fold into the whites with a rubber spatula— or, if you work lightly, you can use a spoon. Bake at 400° F. about 20 minutes.

SERVES 4.

At Serving Time:

Which is instantaneously, of course, sprinkle with superfine sugar and serve with whipped cream or some of the liqueur or spirit that was used to make it.

Variation:

Soufflé Flambé

For Soufflé Flambé, warm ever so slightly about 1/4 cup of the liqueur or rum in a small heatproof ramekin or ladle or porringer; set a match to the liqueur and pour, flaming, over the soufflé.

QUEEN BESS II LEMON SOUFFLÉ

When Queen Elizabeth and Prince Philip visited America in 1959, a fairly small and relatively informal dinner party was arranged for them on the campus of the New Brunswick University at Fredericton. The food was purposely unpretentious and homey. Dessert for so great an occasion could not have been anything other than the "company sweet" of the province, most often called lemon soufflé, but sometimes lemon puff, sponge, or pudding. When warm it is rather like a firm soufflé on top with a lemony sauce on the bottom. When cold, the top is cakelike.

YOU WILL NEED:

1 tablespoon butter or margarine
1/2 cup sugar
2 tablespoons white flour
Grated rind of 1 lemon
3 tablespoons lemon juice
1 tablespoon undiluted frozen orange-
   juice concentrate
2 eggs, separated
1/4 teaspoon salt
1 cup milk

Cream 1 tablespoon butter or margarine with 1/2 cup white sugar and 2 tablespoons white flour. Mix well. Add the grated rind of 1 lemon and 3 tablespoons lemon juice, 1 tablespoon undiluted frozen orange-juice concentrate, 2 egg yolks slightly beaten and 1/4 teaspoon salt. Stir in 1 cup milk. Fold in 2 stiffly beaten egg whites. Pour into a shallow straight-sided baking dish that has been buttered and sugared. Set in pan of hot water and bake 30 minutes at 325° F. or until a silver knife inserted in center comes away clean.

SERVES 4 TO 6.

At Serving Time:

Serve hot or cold.

ORANGE OMELET AU RHUM

Very like a soufflé is a puffy omelet cooked on top of the stove, made with concentrated quick-frozen orange juice flamed with rum and sprinkled with powdered sugar. This is an inspired solution to the problem of nothing-in-the-house-for-dessert.

YOU WILL NEED:

4 eggs, separated
1/2 teaspoon salt
1 tablespoon concentrated quick-
   frozen orange juice
Powdered sugar
4 tablespoons rum

Beat separately yolks and whites of 4 eggs. The yolks should be beaten until thick and daffodil-colored—the whites until stiff. To the yolks add 1/2 teaspoon salt, 1 tablespoon concentrated (undiluted) quick-frozen orange juice. Gently fold in the stiffly beaten whites. Heat an omelet pan or heatproof serving dish. Butter the sides as well as the bottom. Ladle the egg mixture into the pan, cook slowly, but do not lift the edges as for a regular French omelet. As soon as the omelet is puffy and a delicate brown around the edge, place in 375° F. oven or 3 inches away from the broiler in order to brown the top. To judge if the omelet is sufficiently cooked, touch it with your finger. If the finger stays clean it is done.

SERVES 4 TO 6.

At Serving Time:

You need not fold this type of omelet but merely sprinkle with powdered sugar. Slightly warm 4 tablespoons rum, set a match to the rum, and pour blazing around the omelet. Serve immediately.

SOUR CREAM CHERRY PIE

This is a dazzlingly simple and easy version of a famous American specialty!

YOU WILL NEED:

1 frozen cherry pie
1 cup commercial sour cream
1 egg, well beaten
2 tablespoons sugar
1/4 teaspoon salt
1/2 teaspoon vanilla extract
Crumbled macaroons, graham
    crackers, or other cookie crumbs
Cinnamon

Buy a frozen cherry pie and remove the top crust. Warm in the oven. While it is hot, cover with 1 cup commercial sour cream to which you have added 1 well-beaten egg, 2 tablespoons sugar, 1/4 teaspoon salt, and 1/2 teaspoon vanilla extract. Sprinkle lavishly with crumbled macaroons, graham crackers, or any other kind of tasty cookie crumbs.

At Serving Time:

Lightly strew with cinnamon. Serve warm.

MILE-HIGH PIE

YOU WILL NEED:

1 package lemon pie-filling mix
1 tablespoon butter or margarine
1 package pie crust mix or crumb pie
    shell
2 egg whites
1/8 teaspoon salt
1/4 teaspoon cream of tartar
1/4 cup sugar

Make up pie filling according to package directions, but for extra flavor stir into the filling, just after you take it off the stove, 1 tablespoon butter or margarine. Mix well; turn into a baked 8-inch pie shell made from prepared mix or use a crumb crust. To make the meringue, beat until frothy 2 egg whites, 1/8 teaspoon salt, 1/4 teaspoon cream of tartar. Then gradually add 1/4 cup sugar, a little at a time, beating constantly. Continue beating until the meringue is stiff. Top the pie filling with the meringue and bake in a hot oven, 400° F., 8 to 10 minutes.

At Serving Time:

If pie is baked in an attractive pie pan, or one that can be set into a basket, it's a good idea not to try to remove it from the pan because there is always the danger of breaking the crust. The pie will cut better and look more attractive if it is allowed to chill thoroughly before you try to cut it. (Dip knife in hot water. Dry.)

APPLE PIE WITH OLD WILLIAMSBURG SYRUP

YOU WILL NEED:

1 frozen apple pie
Light-brown or maple sugar
Cinnamon or nutmeg
Melted butter or margarine
Maple syrup
2 tablespoons coarsely chopped nuts
Vanilla ice cream

Sprinkle top of a frozen apple pie with a little light-brown or maple sugar and a few grains cinnamon or nutmeg. Heat in the oven. Meanwhile, heat together equal parts melted butter or margarine and maple syrup and add 2 tablespoons coarsely chopped nuts.

At Serving Time:

Pass maple syrup in a small pitcher to be poured at will over the apple pie. A small scoop of vanilla ice cream? Never hurt anyone!

MIRACLE-EASY PLUM PUDDING

This recipe makes a large, dark pudding, not overly rich but wonderfully pungent and delicate. It may be stored in its own mold in the pantry. (If you must reuse the mold, wrap the pudding in aluminum foil.) Freeze, if you wish, or sprinkle with a little liquor and store in a covered crock or tin box.

YOU WILL NEED:

1 package devil's-food cake mix
1 package fruit cake mix
1 egg
2 tablespoons sherry, Madeira, brandy,
    rum, whiskey, or grape juice

Combine 1 package devil's-food cake mix with half the amount of water called for on the package. Add 1 package fruit cake mix, 1 egg, and 2 tablespoons sherry, Madeira, brandy, rum, whiskey, or grape juice. Stir until well blended. Put mixture into a well-buttered 2-pint pudding mold (it should not be more than ²/₃ full). Place mold on rack in pressure cooker; pour boiling water around mold (2¹/₂ cups for 4-quart cooker, 3 to 4 cups for 6-quart cooker) and steam 30 minutes. Reduce pressure instantly.

MAKES A BIG RICH CAKE. ABOUT 20 SERVINGS.

At Serving Time:

Serve flamed with a liquor that matches the one used in the pudding. Pass the traditional hard sauce.

INSTANTANEOUS FRUIT SHERBET

YOU WILL NEED:

1 (6-ounce) can frozen lemonade or
    limeade or ¹/₂ cup cranberry juice
2 heaping cups finely crushed ice

2 egg whites
Sugar (optional)

Put 1 (6-ounce) can frozen lemonade or limeade, partially defrosted, or 1/2 cup cranberry juice with 2 heaping cups finely crushed ice and 2 egg whites into blender. Add sugar if needed. Cover and blend on high speed for 1 minute or until sherbet is consistency of fine snow.

MAKES 1 PINT.

At Serving Time:

Serve immediately in chilled sherbet glasses or keep in trays in the freezer.

COCONUT MACAROONS

YOU WILL NEED:

1 1/2 cups packaged flake coconut
1/2 cup sugar
1 egg, well beaten
1 teaspoon almond extract

Combine 1 1/2 cups packaged flake coconut with 1/2 cup sugar. Mix well. Add 1 well-beaten egg and 1 teaspoon almond extract. Let stand about 5 minutes so that the ingredients will stick together. Drop by teaspoons on a greased cookie sheet and bake in a moderate oven, 350° F., about 15 minutes.

MAKES 1 DOZEN.

At Serving Time:

Serve warm or cold with fruit or ice cream. Delightful when used to top a pudding such as Viennese Chocolate Mousse (see page 207).

LEMON MERINGUE PUDDING WITH BLUEBERRIES

YOU WILL NEED:

2 packages lemon pie filling
1 cup heavy cream, whipped
1 package frozen blueberries
Powdered sugar

Make up 2 packages lemon-pie filling according to directions for lemon pudding. Allow to cool a little. Fold in 1 cup heavy cream, whipped. Pile into an attractive china or glass bowl. Chill in refrigerator ½ hour or more if needed (or in freezer 10 minutes).

SERVES 6.

At Serving Time:

Cover with 1 package thawed and drained frozen blueberries and sprinkle with powdered sugar.

ITALIAN MONTE BIANCO

Monte Bianco, Mont Blanc, or White Mountain—whichever name you use—is a classic continental dessert that will be a source of pride when you serve it. The puree of chestnuts can be bought in cans at quality grocery stores and is worth keeping on hand for those times when you want a quick and glamorous dessert.

YOU WILL NEED:

1 cup sweetened whipped cream
1 (8-ounce) can pureed chestnuts
1 to 2 tablespoons golden rum, vanilla,
    kirsch, or maraschino liqueur
Ready-whipped cream
6 ready-baked meringues (optional)

Combine 1 cup sweetened whipped cream and 1 (8-ounce) can

(1 cup) puree of chestnuts. Flavor to taste with 1 or 2 tablespoons golden rum, vanilla extract, kirsch, or maraschino liqueur. Add flavoring bit by bit to make certain that it does not overpower the taste of the chestnuts.

SERVES 6.

At Serving Time:

Pile lightly in a pyramid on a serving dish. Decorate with ready-whipped cream so that it will look like a snow-capped mountain. If you like, you may buy from the bakeshop ready-baked meringues and set these in a circle around the mountain. Meringues usually come in pairs. Get three pairs and set halves around pyramid.

VIENNESE CHOCOLATE MOUSSE

YOU WILL NEED:

2 tablespoons water
$1/2$ teaspoon instant coffee
1 (6-ounce) package semisweet
   chocolate pieces
$1/4$ teaspoon salt
4 eggs, separated
1 teaspoon vanilla or almond extract or
   2 teaspoons rum or brandy
6 small macaroons (optional)
Whipped cream

In a bowl, put 2 tablespoons water, $1/2$ teaspoon instant coffee, 1 (6-ounce) package semisweet chocolate pieces. Place bowl over hot water and stir until chocolate mixture is melted and blended. Add $1/4$ teaspoon salt. Beat 4 egg yolks until thick and lemon-colored. Add 1 teaspoon vanilla or almond extract or 2 teaspoons rum or brandy. Fold in lightly the whites of 4 eggs beaten until very stiff. Spoon into 6 tiny demitasse cups or small sherry or cocktail glasses. Chill.

SERVES 6.

At Serving Time:

For the true Viennese touch, top each portion with a small macaroon and pass a bowl of whipped cream well flavored with whatever flavoring was used in the pudding, or best of all, with crème de cacão liqueur, using 1 tablespoon liqueur to 1 cup whipped cream.

MIRACLE CHOCOLATE SOUFFLÉ

A package of chocolate tapioca pudding mix can be transformed into a soufflé. The tapioca helps to keep the soufflé high without interfering with its delicacy—the grains do not show or alter the taste. This recipe suggests a way to make the soufflé rise high in the center in the manner of the French restaurateurs. Really wonderful!

YOU WILL NEED:

1 package chocolate tapioca pudding
   mix
6 eggs, separated
1/4 cup sherry or 1 tablespoon brandy
   (optional)
Confectioner's sugar
Milk (as called for in mix)

Make up a package of chocolate tapioca pudding mix according to directions. Add, 1 at a time, 6 egg yolks, beating well after each addition. Then fold in lightly 6 stiffly beaten egg whites. Flavor with 1/4 cup sherry or 1 tablespoon brandy, if desired.

To bake, pour mixture into unbuttered straight-sided baking dish that can come to the table. Pottery is preferred. Fill 7/8 full and make a deep cut all around the soufflé mixture, an inch from the edge. Set in a very hot oven, 425° F., and bake 15 to 20 minutes. This method makes a soufflé with a crusty top and leaves the center soft enough to serve as a sauce.

SERVES 6.

At Serving Time:

Shake a little confectioner's sugar over the top of the soufflé to give it a professional touch and serve instantly. Serves 6.

STRAWBERRY BAVARIAN CREAM

It is important that the ingredients be added exactly in this order or else there will be an overflow.

YOU WILL NEED:

1 (10-ounce) package frozen
   strawberries
2 envelopes unflavored gelatin
1/4 cup milk
2 tablespoons sugar
2 egg yolks or 1 whole egg
1 cup crushed ice
1 cup heavy cream
1 tablespoon sherry or 1 teaspoon
   almond extract

Defrost 1 (10-ounce) package frozen strawberries and drain 1/2 cup of the juice into a saucepan. Heat juice just to simmer. Into blender container put 2 envelopes unflavored gelatin and 1/4 cup cold milk. Add hot strawberry juice, cover and blend for 40 seconds. Add 2 tablespoons sugar, the strawberries, and 2 egg yolks or 1 whole egg, cover and blend for 5 seconds. With motor on, remove cover, add 1 heaping cup crushed ice and 1 cup heavy cream and continue to blend for 20 seconds longer or until dessert begins to thicken. Flavor with 1 tablespoon sherry or 1 teaspoon almond extract.

SERVES 6 TO 8.

At Serving Time:

Decorate with strawberries and almonds.

CRÊPES

These are very different from griddle cakes—much thinner and of a different texture. Pancake mixes do not work very well for this type of cake although you will find recipes listed on many packages. The batter is very simple to make yourself, and incidentally this is one place where you need not bother sifting the flour. Use it as it comes.

YOU WILL NEED:

³/₄ cup all-purpose flour
¹/₂ teaspoon salt
1 cup milk
2 eggs
Salad oil
Sugar
Cinnamon (optional)

Put ³/₄ cup flour and ¹/₂ teaspoon salt into a bowl. Make a well in the center and pour in 1 cup milk and 2 eggs. Stir and beat until perfectly smooth. Batter should be as thin as coffee cream. If necessary, add a little extra milk. Heat a 5-inch frying pan. Pour in a few drops of salad oil and tip so that the bottom of the pan glistens with a thin film of oil. Pour in 2 or 3 tablespoons batter— just enough to cover the pan thinly. Tilt so that mixture spreads evenly. Cook on one side. Turn and cook on the other side.

MAKES ABOUT 18.

At Serving Time:

Sprinkle with sugar or sugar and cinnamon. Roll up or fold in quarters and arrange on hot platter.

Variation:

Maple Pancakes

Brush the pancakes with melted butter. Sprinkle with maple sugar. Roll and serve 2 or 3 per portion on a heated plate with a section of lemon, which can be squeezed on the pancakes.

CRÊPES SUZETTE JUBILEE

These "crêpes" are in truth frozen cherry blintzes.

YOU WILL NEED:

2 (5-ounce) packages frozen cherry
 blintzes
1/4 cup orange marmalade
1/4 cup red currant jelly
2 tablespoons hot water
2 tablespoons brandy
1 cup canned pitted black cherries,
 drained

Heat 2 (5-ounce) packages frozen cherry blintzes according to directions. Combine 1/4 cup each orange marmalade and red currant jelly with 2 tablespoons hot water. Stir until melted. Add 2 tablespoons brandy and 1 cup canned pitted black cherries, drained. Heat and stir 2 minutes.

SERVES 3 TO 4.

At Serving Time:

Pour hot sauce over blintzes.

ZABAIONE

This famous Italian dessert is highly controversial as to the spelling, the technique, and the ingredients. Sometimes it is spelled "sabayon"; more often "zabaione" or "zabaglione."

The traditional wine to use is Italian Marsala, but a moderately sweet sherry, Madeira, or rum may be used. If you use rum—only half as much.

Zabaione is served either warm in warmed stemmed glasses, or chilled. Often it is used as a sauce over cake, pudding, or fruits.

The classic recipes call only for egg yolks. But we learned from no less an authority than Mama Laura (of Mama Laura's own notable restaurant in New York) that adding a couple of whites to half a dozen yolks makes a lighter, more delicate and elegant dessert.

This recipe is close to miraculous because it requires no cooking whatsoever. All you do is heat the wine.

YOU WILL NEED:

³/₄ cup Marsala, sherry, or Madeira, or
  ¹/₃ cup rum
6 egg yolks (or 4 egg yolks and 2 whole
  eggs)
6 tablespoons sugar

Heat to boiling point ³/₄ cup Marsala, sherry, or Madeira, or ¹/₃ cup rum. Place in glass container of blender 6 egg yolks or 4 egg yolks and 2 whole eggs. Add 6 tablespoons sugar. Cover and blend just about 5 seconds, just enough to mix the eggs and the sugar. It is important not to blend too much. While the blender is still running, remove cover and slowly pour in the hot wine. As soon as the last drop is added the zabaione should be foamy and thick, ready to use. If for any reason it should not seem quite thick enough, you can go back to the old method and heat it at 200° F. or in the top of a double boiler. Stir constantly! Remove from heat as soon as it begins to look puffy.

SERVES 4.

At Serving Time:

Pour into 4 warmed wine or champagne glasses. Serve with ladyfingers or macaroons. Or chill and serve plain or with fruits; i.e., peaches, strawberries, or pears, fresh or poached. Can also be used as a sauce—warm or cold—and poured over ice cream, cake, or puddings.

BOURBON BALLS

For some families, including ours, Christmas wouldn't be Christmas without these balls.

YOU WILL NEED:

12 to 15 vanilla wafers
1 cup chopped pecans
1 cup powdered sugar
2 tablespoons cocoa
$1/2$ tablespoons white corn syrup
$1/4$ cup bourbon

Blend 12 to 15 vanilla wafers until they make fine crumbs. Measure to be sure you have 1 cup vanilla wafer crumbs (graham crackers or other plain cookies may also be used). Place in a good-sized bowl, along with 1 cup chopped pecans, 1 cup powdered sugar, and 2 tablespoons cocoa. Add to dry ingredients $1/2$ tablespoon white corn syrup, which has been stirred up with about $1/4$ cup bourbon. The mixture should be moist enough to form readily into balls. If it isn't, another dribble of bourbon! To lend an extra aromatic savor, moisten your hands with bourbon when making the balls. Roll balls marble-size in powdered or confectioner's sugar. Keep cool until ready to serve.

MAKES ABOUT 4 DOZEN.

CRÈME BRULÉE (BROILED CREAM)

This rich custard gets a topping of cracking-crisp brown sugar. The old recipes call for scalding the cream, cooking over warm water, setting the pan into cracked ice, using an iron salamander, but we translate it into the blender, the thermostatically controlled frying pan or saucepan, the freezing compartment of your refrigerator, and the electric broiler.

YOU WILL NEED:

6 eggs
3/4 cup light-brown sugar or 6
   tablespoons white sugar
3 cups light cream
Salt
Nutmeg
Light-brown sugar

In the blender place 6 eggs, 3/4 cup light-brown sugar, or 6 tablespoons white sugar, 3 cups light cream, a pinch of salt, and a sprinkle of freshly grated nutmeg. Blend until light and creamy, but not too frothy, about 15 seconds. Cook at 200° F., stirring constantly, until the mixture coats a silver spoon. Pour into 6 to 8 custard cups or ramekins and set on a cookie sheet in the freezing compartment until cool, stirring once or twice. Remove and sprinkle at least 1/4-inch deep with light-brown sugar so that no custard shows. Set under the broiler until sugar melts, watching every second to be sure it does not burn. Put back into the refrigerator. The top will congeal into a shiny crust, like the clear part of peanut brittle.

SERVES 6 TO 8.

At Serving Time:

It is customary to give the crust a slight whack with a fork or knife to shatter it in the center, probably to make it easier to get at the lovely cream underneath.

Variations:

Creamless Crème Brulée

Instead of light cream you may use 3 cups milk and 3 tablespoons butter—all of it goes into the blender together.

EASIEST CRÈME BRULÉE

Instead of basic ingredients, use an instant vanilla pudding mix and blend in 2 egg yolks. You do not need to bother to cook anything. Simply follow package directions. Chilling is unnecessary, of course. Simply cover the pudding with light-brown sugar and proceed as above.

Note: In all creme brulee recipes it is important not to have any lumps, for they make large dark blotches. Some people sieve the sugar, but it isn't necessary. If sugar is lumpy, give it a whirl in the blender.

COEUR FLOTTANTE À LA RITZ

At the old Ritz Carlton and later at the Carlton House in New York, floating hearts were a favorite dessert.

YOU WILL NEED:

1 (3-ounce) package lemon gelatin
3 cups custard sauce (see below)
Apricots, strawberries, peaches, or
    other fruits
1/3 cup sherry or Madeira

Prepare lemon-flavored gelatin and whip following package directions. Spoon into 1-quart heart-shaped mold, chilled or rinsed in cold water. Swift-chill in freezer 15 minutes by timer and keep in refrigerator until ready to serve.

Have ready 3 cups custard sauce made swiftly by adding 1 cup milk to a can of custard pudding, or make custard sauce by adding 3 instead of 2 cups milk to a package of custard pudding mix. Flavor sauce with 1/3 cup sherry or Madeira.

SERVES 6 TO 8.

At Serving Time:

Unmold upon a wine-flavored custard sauce in which you have hidden halved apricots, strawberries, sliced peaches, or any other delicate fruit.

IMPROMPTU APRICOT TARTS

YOU WILL NEED:

3 English muffins, split
Melted–
6 tablespoons brown sugar
1/2 to 3/4 cup ready-whipped cream
Frozen apricot halves, thawed and
   drained
Whipped cream

Split 3 English muffins, removing most of the soft inside. Brush with melted butter and sprinkle each half with 1 tablespoon brown sugar. Toast under broiler. These are your tart shells. Place 1 or 2 tablespoons ready-whipped cream on each shell. Cover with frozen apricot halves, which have been thawed and drained, round side up. Garnish with whipped cream.

SERVES 6.

GLAZED STRAWBERRY TARTS

Many bakeshops will, if you ask them, make up for you either puff paste or pie crust shells for tarts. In some specialty food shops you can buy already baked tart shells. For this delicious dessert and many others, your own cracker-crumb crust may be used. The rest is wonderfully easy. You will note that a professional-looking glaze is given to the fruit by the simple expedient of melting bought currant jelly.

YOU WILL NEED:

6 small or 4 large tart shells
4 to 6 tablespoons ready-whipped
   cream
1 pint fresh or 1 (12-ounce) package
   quick-frozen strawberries
1/2 cup currant jelly

Into the bottom of 6 small or 4 large tart shells place a tablespoon of ready-whipped cream. On top of the cream, arrange large fresh or drained whole quick-frozen strawberries. Melt gently over very low heat 1/2 cup currant jelly and pour carefully over the berries. Chill.

MAKES 6.

At Serving Time:

Arrange tarts on a serving plate. Garnish with green leaves.

UNCOOKED HOT-FUDGE SAUCE

If you like a bittersweet chocolate flavor you will not add the sugar.

YOU WILL NEED:

1 (6-ounce) package chocolate bits
2 tablespoons superfine sugar
1/2 cup hot coffee

Place 1 (6-ounce) package chocolate bits into blender. Cover and blend for 6 seconds. Scrape chocolate away from the sides of container with a spatula. Add 2 tablespoons superfine sugar and 1/2 cup steaming hot coffee. Cover and blend for 10 seconds longer.

MAKES 1/2 CUP.

At Serving Time:

This goes on any sort of cake as well as ice cream or puddings.

INSTANT VANILLA SAUCE

YOU WILL NEED:

3 cups milk
1 package instant vanilla pudding
1/2 teaspoon pure vanilla extract or a 2-
    inch piece vanilla bean

Place in the blender 3 cups milk, 1 package instant vanilla pudding, 1/2 teaspoon pure vanilla extract or a 2-inch piece of vanilla bean. Blend about 40 seconds.

MAKES 3 CUPS.

At Serving Time:

Pass in a pitcher or sauce boat with snow pudding or with gelatin desserts. Also good on fruit or cake.

Variations:

Instant Butterscotch Sauce

Use a package of butterscotch instant pudding. Flavor with rum or rum extract instead of vanilla.

Instant Chocolate Sauce

Use a package of instant chocolate-pudding mix and if you like a mocha flavor, add 1 teaspoon instant coffee or a couple of drops of Angostura bitters.

LIME CHIFFON PIE

YOU WILL NEED:

2 packages lime-flavored gelatin
2 cups hot water
3 eggs, separated

1 (6-ounce) can limeade concentrate
Crumb crust of chocolate wafers,
    graham crackers, or ginger wafers
Whipped cream
Shaved or grated chocolate or
    chocolate shot

Dissolve 2 packages lime-flavored gelatin dessert in 2 cups hot water. Beat until light and lemon-colored 3 egg yolks and 1 (6-ounce) can limeade concentrate. Combine with the gelatin. (Your electric blender is perfect for the job.) Swift-chill in freezer about 15 minutes or until set around the edges, still quivery in the center. Add 3 unbeaten egg whites and whip with electric beater at low speed until very light and fluffy. Place in a crumb crust made of chocolate wafers, graham crackers, or ginger wafers. Swift-chill 10 to 15 minutes longer in the freezer. Keep in refrigerator until needed.

SERVES 8 TO 10.

At Serving Time:

Cover with a thin layer of whipped cream, shaved or grated chocolate, or chocolate shot.

RUSSIAN PASKA

This is a traditional dish for Russian Easter but it is delightful to serve as a not-too-sweet dessert with coffee cake or sweet rolls at any time of the year.

YOU WILL NEED:

12 ounces cream cheese
3/4 cup light cream
2 tablespoons cognac
2 egg yolks, hard-cooked
1/4 cup chopped almonds
1/2 cup mixed glacéed fruits and peels

Place in the bowl of your electric mixer 12 ounces cream cheese, 3/4 cup light cream, and 2 tablespoons cognac. Mix until very smooth. Add the chopped yolks of 2 hard-cooked eggs, 1/4 cup chopped almonds, 1/2 cup mixed glacéed fruits and peels. Line a quart-size mold or clay flower pot with dampened cheesecloth. Pack the mixture into the mold or simply mold into a pyramid with your hands and wrap in waxed paper. Cover. Chill in the refrigerator several hours or overnight.

MAKES 12 TO 18 SERVINGS.

At Serving Time:

Turn out on a plate and decorate with leaves and flowers. For Easter, the Greek Orthodox set a birthday candle in the center.

Fruits—with Flair

When in doubt, serve fruit. Fresh, quick-frozen, or canned, raw or cooked, plain or glamorized in any number of tempting ways, fruit is almost everybody's favorite dessert. So many different kinds of fruits and berries in so many different guises are now available, quick-frozen or canned, that it is sad to confine your attention entirely to old favorites. Have you, for instance, heard of the many forms in which the apple is being packed—in slices for pies and puddings, cubed and sweetened for compotes, as applesauce, sweetened or unsweetened, baked apples, too, in cans or quick-frozen? Now all year round you can have your favorite fresh berry desserts with quick-frozen strawberries, blackberries, blueberries, boysenberries, cherries, loganberries, and youngberries, too. Be sure to include them in your menu plans.

And when you serve the standbys—canned peaches, pears, cherries, and pineapple—present them imaginatively. A touch of vanilla or almond extract added to the syrup, a little brandy or wine, a frosty sauce made of whipped vanilla ice cream. All these can lend variety. Be wary, though, and do not overpower the delicate flavor of fruit with too much flavoring or trimming. The recipes that follow pursue a judicious middle course.

BAKED APPLES GARNI

Baked apples can be bought either canned or quick-frozen, generally 3 or

4 apples to a can or carton. There are a number of ways to dress up these apples to make them look and taste homemade.

YOU WILL NEED:

Baked apples (1 per serving)
Red cinnamon candies or red pure-
  food coloring
Cinnamon
Lemon juice
Lemon peel (optional)
Heavy cream

Place apples in buttered heatproof glass pie plate or other shallow serving dish. Drop into the center of each apple 2 or 3 red cinnamon candies, or add to the syrup from the apples a few drops red pure-food coloring and sprinkle apples with cinnamon and a few drops lemon juice, using about 1/2 teaspoon on each apple. A twist of lemon peel may be put in the center of the apples, too, or laid over the top. Pour about 1/2 inch apple liquid from can or package, or 1/2 inch water into the bottom of the baking dish. Cover and allow to heat in a hot oven, 400° F., about 10 minutes or until warm.

At Serving Time:

These are most delicious when served warm with a pitcher of plain heavy cream. However, you may use whipped cream if you like.

Variations:

Baked Apples with Orange

Into the center of each apple, place 1 teaspoon undiluted quick-frozen concentrated orange juice.

Baked Apples Porcupine

Set 4 well-drained baked apples in baking dish. Cover each apple completely with a stiff meringue made by beating the whites of 2 eggs with 2 tablespoons sugar. Meringue may be flavored with 1/2 teaspoon vanilla. Stick almond halves all over the meringue porcupine-fashion. Sprinkle lightly with granulated sugar. Place in a moderate oven, 350° F., 5 minutes. Then increase the heat to 400° F., and bake 5 minutes longer or until delicately brown. Do not put any liquid in the bottom of the pan.

PEACH AMBROSIA

The traditional ambrosia of the South is made of oranges, but this delightful variant uses canned or quick-frozen sliced peaches in place of them.

YOU WILL NEED:

2 cups canned or quick-frozen sliced
   peaches, drained (reserve juice)
1 cup shredded coconut
1 tablespoon lemon juice or 2
   tablespoons sherry or white port

Drain canned or quick-frozen sliced peaches. Save juice. Arrange in a glass bowl suitable for serving. Alternate layers of peaches and shredded coconut. For 2 cups peaches, use about 1 cup shredded coconut. Add to the juice of the peaches 1 tablespoon lemon juice or 2 tablespoons sherry or white port. Sprinkle over peaches and coconut.

SERVES 4.

At Serving Time:

This dessert may be served as soon as it is made, an advantage over the old-fashioned ambrosia that had to stand for several hours at least in order to blend the flavors.

Variation:

One cup sliced bananas, oranges, or diced pineapple may be added to the peaches. Increase coconut to 1¹/₂ cups.

SERVES 6.

PINEAPPLE ROYALE

For a party nothing could be more impressive than this Escoffier dessert. You must choose a pretty pineapple with a well-shaped topknot of leaves.

YOU WILL NEED:

1 large pineapple with leaves
1 can or 1 package quick-frozen fruit
    salad or fruit cocktail, drained
2 tablespoons kirsch, brandy,
    Cointreau, or Grand Marnier
Canned peach halves
1 large fresh or quick-frozen
    strawberries or blueberries
Confectioner's sugar

Cut off top of the pineapple with the bunch of leaves and set aside in a safe place. Scoop out pineapple, leaving a wall about 1/2-inch thick all around and at the bottom. Cut fresh pineapple into small pieces and combine with 1 can (or 1 package frozen) fruit cocktail or fruit salad, drained. (The pieces of fruit are larger in fruit salad.) Sprinkle with 2 tablespoons kirsch, brandy, Cointreau, or Grand Marnier. Place fruit in pineapple shell. Set pineapple top in place, and if you wish to follow the great tradition, surround the base of pineapple with canned peach halves and large fresh or quick-frozen strawberries or blueberries.

At Serving Time:

Decorate with shiny green leaves. (Violet or rose leaves are particularly appropriate.) If desired, a little liquor such as is used to flavor the fruits may be sprinkled lightly over the canned peaches. A slight frosting of confectioner's sugar over leaves and fruit is effective (for looks only). The number of servings depends upon the sizes of the cans and the number of fruits used.

WHOLE BAKED BANANAS FLAMBÉ

YOU WILL NEED:

4 bananas
Confectioner's sugar
1/2 cup golden rum

Place whole, not-too-ripe unpeeled bananas, 1 for each serving, in a shallow baking dish—preferably one that can be brought to the table. Bake 30 minutes in a moderate oven, 350° F.

SERVES 4.

At Serving Time:

At the table, or if you prefer, before you bring the dish to the table, pull back 1 section of skin on each banana, sprinkle bananas with confectioner's sugar, and pour over them 1/2 cup slightly warmed golden rum, which has been set ablaze with a match. The guests spoon the banana out of it shell just as one eats a baked potato.

COMPOTE OF MELON BALLS

YOU WILL NEED:

1/2 cup sugar
2 packages frozen melon balls

A fast, distinguished way to present frozen melon balls: bring to a boil 1/2 cup sugar and 1/2 cup water. Cook 2 minutes. Add 2 packages frozen melon balls. Remove from heat; cover and allow to stand. In a few minutes the melon balls will be thawed and the compote ready to serve.

SERVES 4.

ROSY RHUBARB COMPOTE

Outside of a few top restaurants, it is practically impossible to discover a properly put together rhubarb compote, or as it is more mundanely known, stewed rhubarb. Almost always the fruit is cooked to shreds, the glow gone. It is either set-your-teeth-on-edge sour or syrupy sweet. This recipe, which I learned in France, achieves perfection every time. The rhubarb is firm but tender. There is just the right amount of sweetness.

YOU WILL NEED:

1/2 cup sugar
1/4 teaspoon salt
Rhubarb, 1 package frozen,
    or 1 pound fresh, cut up
Red food coloring (optional)

Combine 1/2 cup water, 1/2 cup sugar, and 1/4 teaspoon salt. Bring to a boil and cook a minute or two until the syrup is bright and clear. Add 1 package frozen rhubarb. Bring to a boil again. There should be bubbles all over the pot, even in the center. Cook no more than a minute or two, moving the pieces around so that they cook evenly. Do this with a fork; never with a spoon. Cover closely, remove from heat, and allow to stand until ready to serve, warm or chilled. If the rhubarb is not sufficiently pink, add 2 or 3 drops red food coloring.

SERVES 3 TO 4.

STRAWBERRIES ROMANOFF

In strawberry season all over the world, the most famous restaurants feature—each with its own variation—this classic combination of fine strawberries, orange juice, Curaçao, and cream. To achieve the most dramatic effect, arrange the makings on a tray and put the dessert together at the table.

YOU WILL NEED:

1 pint whole fresh or frozen
   strawberries
1 cup orange juice
1 pint vanilla ice cream
¹/₄ cup Curaçao, Cointreau, Grand
   Marnier, or brandy

Arrange on a tray an attractive bowlful of strawberries. If you use quick-frozen berries, have them almost but not completely thawed. To 1 pint berries add 1 cup orange juice. Also have on hand a bowl of vanilla ice cream—about a pint—and a bottle of Curaçao. Provide yourself also with a fork and a large spoon for serving.

SERVES 6.

At Serving Time:

Stir and soften vanilla ice cream with a fork. Add ¹/₄ cup Curaçao (Cointreau, Grand Marnier, or brandy may also be used). Stir into the ice cream. Serve strawberries on chilled plates and top each portion with a couple of spoonfuls of the liqueur-flavored ice cream.

Timesaving Beverages

Instant tea, coffee, and chocolate are certainly here to stay. Convenient and economical, in many busy households they have already become indispensable. Suggested in this chapter are a number of ways to serve instant beverages to the best advantage.

A number of party drinks—punches and nogs—are included. Each is a shortcut recipe using either canned, bottled, or quick-frozen fruit juices, or in some cases, sherbet or ice cream, bought or made from a mix.

One point cannot be overemphasized: Hot drinks should be hot, hot, hot. Whenever possible, demitasse cups should be heated. Simply place them in an oven set at not more than 200° F.

Cold drinks must be cold, cold, cold. If you are giving a party, you may find yourself faced with an ice-cube shortage. You can, of course, freeze ice cubes ahead of time, emptying and saving the cubes in bowls in the refrigerator until needed, but there is an easier way. In cities and in medium-sized towns you will find listed in the classified section of your telephone directory one or more ice companies that will deliver to you in cartons—at no great expense—any quantity of ice cubes, as well as shaved or finely crushed ice so necessary for juleps, frozen daiquiris, cobblers, and the like. They will also send you large chunks of ice for your punch bowl.

On the subject of punch-bowl ice, those of you who are fortunate enough to have a freezing compartment in your refrigerator or a deep-freeze can make your own ice blocks simply by freezing water in a bowl, mold, or deep pan. If you wish, you may decorate the ice by placing in the water, before freezing, flowers, leaves, or fruits. Imagine the drama provided by a bunch of grapes frozen into a block of ice!

COFFEE FOR GOURMETS

All over the world there are people who swear "on the sacred beards of their ancestors" that coffee must be ground at the moment you use it. Of course there are grinders and grinders, hand and electric. The blender does an excellent job if, and this is a large if, it is one of the big and most expensive so-called custom multispeed models with extra-large blades and plenty of power. The smaller, lighter blenders are quickly ruined if you use them as coffee grinders.

With the proper blender you need buy only one type of coffee in the bean, and you can grind it fresh for any kind of coffee-making just by timing. Naturally, large amounts of coffee take longer to grind, but here are approximate timings:

1. For the old-fashioned open-pot method known as boiled or steeped coffee—3/4 cup whole coffee beans will be properly ground in about 10 seconds.
2. For the percolator—12 to 15 seconds.
3. Drip coffee—35 to 40 seconds.
4. Very fine drip for Chemex, etc.—50 seconds.
5. Pulverized coffee for making Turkish coffee—60 to 65 seconds.

CAFÉ ROYALE

This simple trick will most certainly add a gala note to any occasion. Serve demitasse in the usual fashion and provide rum, brandy, or Grand Marnier. Each person flames his own coffee like this: The coffee spoon is dipped into the coffee to be warmed. Then the spoon is rested on the rim of the coffee cup. A lump of sugar goes into the spoon and over the sugar is poured a little liquor. Set a match to the liquor. (If the liquor is slightly warmed beforehand, you are certain to have a good blaze.) Let it flame up for a minute or so and drop the flaming sugar into the cup. For those who do not like sugar in their coffee the liquor may be flamed in the spoon without sugar. This ceremony is most effective if the room is darkened.

INSTANT DEMITASSE

Some connoisseurs still object to instant coffee but because it is so easy, so quick, and so economical, its use is becoming more and more widespread. There are a number of ways by which one may add full body and a stronger flavor to an instant demitasse.

YOU WILL NEED:

Instant coffee (see below for
   measurements)

By using standard measurements—a measuring cup and a measuring spoon—you can be assured of uniform quality in your demitasse. For instance, to make 6 servings, pour 2 measuring cups of actively boiling water on 2 level measuring tablespoons of instant coffee. Stir to assure a brew of even strength. To make 12 servings, use 4 measuring cups of water and 4 level measuring tablespoons of instant coffee. Prize Hint: Add instant coffee to cold water; bring to a boil and boil for 30 seconds. The difference is amazing.

At Serving Time:

According to tradition, demitasse is generally served in the living room after dinner, but since most of us do not have special dining rooms nowadays, many hostesses prefer to bring the demitasse to the table and serve it along with the dessert. To keep the coffee piping hot, set the coffeepot over a candle warmer. These are available at most department store houseware counters now and are quite inexpensive. The candle flame is not hot enough to harm even a thin china coffeepot.

Variation:

Demitasse with Cinnamon Stick

Into each demitasse cup, place a stick of cinnamon to be used as a stirrer. The cinnamon stick looks attractive and adds a delicate flavor to the coffee.

CAFÉ DIABLE

Special pans, burners, and ladles are available for making and serving this most dramatic of after-dinner coffees, but it can be done very effectively with any chafing dish.

YOU WILL NEED:

1½ cups brandy
Peel of ½ orange
Peel of ½ lemon
10 lumps sugar
4 cloves
1 cinnamon stick
2 cups instant demitasse

Heat but do not boil in a chafing dish or Café Diable pan 1½ cups brandy along with the thin outer peel of ½ orange and ½ lemon, 8 lumps sugar, 4 cloves, and 1 stick of cinnamon. Warm a small ladle by holding a match under it or hold it over the candle flame. Dip up about 2 tablespoons of the spice-brandy mixture and place 2 sugar lumps in the ladle. Set fire to the sugar. Lower the blazing spiced brandy into the bowl, which will blaze up in its turn, and while it is blazing pour in 2 measuring cups instant demitasse.

SERVES 8 TO 10.

At Serving Time:

All the above should, of course, be done with some ceremony at the dinner table in a darkened room. Ladle the Cafe Diable into tiny coffee cups after the flame has died down.

COFFEE COBBLER

In Europe many wines and liqueurs are served in small glasses over shaved or finely crushed ice. This is an attractive way to serve demitasse on a warm summer evening. Fill sherry or cocktail glasses with very finely crushed or shaved ice. Pour over the ice instant demitasse. Top with a swirl of ready-whipped cream and decorate with a bit of glazed fruit. Serve with short straws, made by cutting ordinary ice-cream soda straws into 2 or 3 pieces.

COFFEE FOR A THRONG

YOU WILL NEED:

10 quarts water
1 pound drip-grind coffee
2 cheesecloth bags
String

Remove load-and-lift rack and pour 10 quarts water into inset pan of roaster oven. Set temperature control at 250° F. Tie 1 pound drip-grind coffee loosely in two cheesecloth bags and place in water. Cover roaster. When light goes out, turn control to 160° F. Let stand 10 minutes. Remove coffee bags. Stir and serve or keep hot at 250°.

MAKES ABOUT 50 SERVINGS.

At Serving Time:
Dip into coffee cups or pour into heated coffeepots.

VIENNESE COFFEE

It is traditional in Vienna and all through the Austrian Tyrol to serve strong, hot coffee topped with whipped cream not only after dinner but at any time during the day. Make up instant demitasse for 6. In an attractive chilled bowl, pass ready-whipped cream delicately flavored, if desired, with a little brandy or liqueur. Instead of whipped cream, vanilla ice cream may be passed in the bowl. This should be softened with a fork and flavored with brandy, rum, or liqueur. Use 1 tablespoon of liqueur to 1 cup of whipped cream or ice cream.

FLAMING TEA BOWL

On a cold winter evening, after skiing or just walking, nothing could be more appropriate than this hot and spicy drink. It has the further virtue of being inexpensive and very easy to prepare.

YOU WILL NEED:

1 quart hot tea
1 thinly sliced lemon
4 teaspoons honey
1 cup golden rum
Cinnamon sticks (optional)

To a quart of hot tea made from your very best tea add 1 thinly sliced lemon and 4 teaspoons honey. Stir well.

SERVES 6 TO 8.

At Serving Time:

Bring punch to the table in a chafing dish or a casserole that will fit over a candle warmer so that it will keep blazing hot. Warm separately but do not boil 1 cup golden rum. Set rum ablaze with a match. Pour into the hot tea and ladle into cups or mugs. If you have them you may put cinnamon sticks in the cups for stirrers.

JAMAICA COGNAC GRANITO

In a tattered book published by the Beacon Hill Press of Boston, way back in the thirties, we found a glorious tall cool drink called, for no reason that we fathom, a Jamaica Cognac Granito. But Granito is an Italian ice. Cognac is not native to Jamaica. But evidently Jamaicans know a good thing when they taste it!

YOU WILL NEED:

Lemon or orange ice
1 jigger (3 tablespoons) cognac
1 tablespoon Curaçao
Sparkling water
Grating of nutmeg
Sprig of mint

Fill a tall, iced-tea glass ¹/₃ full of lemon or orange ice. Pour in 1 jigger (3 tablespoons) cognac, 1 tablespoon Curaçao. Fill with sparkling water. Stir. A grating of nutmeg goes on top.

SERVES 1.

At Serving Time:

Add a sprig of mint.

BANANA FRUIT PUNCH

YOU WILL NEED:

1 (6-ounce) can orange-juice or lime-
    juice or pineapple-juice concentrate
3 ripe bananas
2 tablespoons grenadine syrup

Reconstitute frozen orange-juice, lime-juice, or pineapple-juice concentrate according to directions, adding 3 mashed ripe bananas and 2 tablespoons grenadine syrup. This is most easily done in an electric blender.

SERVES 6 TO 8.

At Serving Time:

Serve very cold in tall glasses, garnished with fruit.

WEDDING-RING PUNCH

YOU WILL NEED:

1 (6-ounce) can frozen orange juice
1 (6-ounce) can frozen lemonade
4 to 6 quarts chilled ginger ale
Mint leaves

Defrost 1 (6-ounce) can frozen orange juice and 1 (6-ounce) can frozen lemonade, and add water as directed on cans. Combine orange juice and lemonade and pour into 2-quart ring mold. Freeze 24 hours.

MAKES 32 TO 48 ½-CUP SERVINGS.

At Serving Time:

Unmold ring into center of large punch bowl. Pour 4 to 6 quarts chilled ginger ale into bowl at the edge so that the wedding ring floats to the top. Decorate with mint leaves.

HOLIDAY NOG

Instead of going to all the bother of beating egg yolks, egg whites, and cream for an eggnog party, try this very simple and most delicious recipe made with ice cream from the corner store.

YOU WILL NEED:

1 pint vanilla ice cream
2 cups rye or bourbon whiskey
1 cup golden rum
1 cup milk
Nutmeg

Place 1 pint vanilla ice cream in a bowl. Pour over it 2 cups rye or bourbon whiskey, 1 cup golden rum, and 1 cup milk. Beat with a rotary egg beater until the ice cream is almost melted and the nog is foamy.

SERVES 6.

At Serving Time:

Ladle into small punch cups and sprinkle with grated nutmeg.

WASSAIL

On Christmas Eve, New Year's, or Twelfth Night, the Wassail Bowl is traditional.

YOU WILL NEED:

12 canned baked apples
3 quarts apple juice
1 teaspoon vanilla
1 cinnamon stick
1 whole cracked nutmeg or $1/2$
   teaspoon ground nutmeg
Lemon rind
2 teaspoons whole cloves
2 tablespoons honey or brown sugar
   (optional)
About 1 pint brandy or applejack

Warm 12 canned baked apples in the oven, providing 1 for each guest. To 3 quarts apple juice add 1 teaspoon vanilla, 1 stick cinnamon, 2 teaspoons whole cloves, 1 whole cracked nutmeg or $1/2$ teaspoon ground nutmeg, and a little thin lemon rind. Also, if desired, add 2 tablespoons honey or brown sugar. Simmer for a few minutes. Pour while hot into punch bowl.

SERVES 12.

At Serving Time:

Place a baked apple in each mug. Pour on 1 jigger (3 tablespoons) brandy or applejack that has been slightly warmed. Set aflame and ladle the spiced apple juice over the baked apple. Serve with a spoon.

Variation

Wassail for the Young

Even without brandy or applejack, Wassail can be a very festive drink. Simply omit liquor.

Index